TRUE THAI, with its thoughtful recipes and arresting photographs, brings the bright and enchanting spirit of Thailand to life. It is a feast for the eyes and the imagination—a pleasure both to read and to cook from.

—JAMES OSELAND, editor-in-chief of
Rodale's Organic Life and author of *Cradle of Flavor*

Chef Hong Thaimee has become a voice for authentic, modern Thai cuisine and an influencer in the culinary industry. Without a doubt, I will soon be making one of her recipes.

—JEAN-GEORGES VONGERICHTEN, from his Foreword

TRUE THAI is pulsating with flavor, color, and passion. The love to which this book is dedicated comes through on every page—a bold welcome to Hong Thaimee's table. TRUE THAT!

—ANITA LO, Annisa

TRUE THAI

REAL FLAVORS FOR EVERY TABLE

HONG THAIMEE

FOREWORD BY
JEAN-GEORGES AND CEDRIC VONGERICHTEN

PHOTOGRAPHS BY
NOAH FECKS AND PAUL WAGTOUICZ

RIZZOLI
NEW YORK

New York · Paris · London · Milan

TO
LOVE,
THE BEST
INGREDIENT

CONTENTS

FOREWORD

Southeast Asia is where I began my love affair with Asian food. At the age of twenty-three, I traveled to Bangkok to assume the role of *chef de cuisine* at the Oriental Hotel. Immediately upon visiting the Aw Taw Kaw market, I fell in love with the local flavors and became obsessed with ingredients like lemongrass, chiles, and ginger. Since that visit, my cooking has evolved from classical French cuisine to dishes that rarely exclude the flavors I discovered on that trip.

Hong Thaimee applied for a hostess position at Spice Market, but immediately talked her way into the kitchen. I noticed her talent and became interested in what she had to offer. The first time Hong ever cooked for me, she made pad thai. My first bite transported me back to my days spent in Thailand. Her flavors were perfectly balanced, and from that moment I knew this dish would become her claim to fame. After a short hiatus, Hong returned to work with us at Perry St. With everything she had to offer, it was a no-brainer to welcome her back into the kitchen and into our restaurant family.

Every so often, a star shines in one of my kitchens. Although every individual who works at one of my restaurants is talented, there are some who stand out among the crowd. These are the individuals who are going to make a difference in the culinary world. They know how to enhance food and turn it into a work of art. Their hands create cravings that last a lifetime. From the moment I tasted Hong Thaimee's cooking, I knew she was one of these people.

As I turn the pages of her cookbook, I am reminded once again of her talent. She has become a voice for authentic, modern Thai cuisine and an influencer in the culinary industry. Without a doubt, I will soon be making one of her recipes from this book. And I hope that one day she will again make me the pad thai that I have been craving ever since the first time I tried it!

—JEAN-GEORGES VONGERICHTEN

I was born in Thailand, when my father was a chef at the Oriental Hotel. We stayed there until I was two years old. I don't remember much, but I feel my connection with Thai food must stem from my mother eating Thai food every day when I was in her belly. In my kitchen, we use a lot of Thai ingredients, from lemongrass, ginger, and kaffir lime to Thai chiles and coconut milk. It is such an electrifying cuisine, and I can't get enough of it.

The first time Hong cooked for me was at Perry St. On that day, she spent almost an hour in the hallway of the building's basement, seated on the floor, preparing essential Thai ingredients like lemongrass, kaffir, and red Thai chiles by crushing them in a mortar. For a moment, I thought I was in Thailand. She was making a curry from scratch, and the hallway smelled incredible. Hong cooks with her heart and with true Thai flavor. That night, the whole kitchen crew feasted, with some of the cooks having their first genuine experience of Thai cooking.

After spending time in the kitchen at Spice Market and in the kitchen line at Perry St, Hong became very enthusiastic about opening her own restaurant. One day she told me, "Chef, it was great working for you, but I am going to open my own place." I was very happy for her; starting a restaurant is tough, but I knew she would be successful.

In *True Thai*, Hong shares her food journey, from her childhood in Thailand, including family recipes, to New York City; from what inspired her to become a chef to her passion to share her cuisine with the world. She shows how to make easy and high-impact flavor at home. This is real *True Thai* flavor, and I recommend it to everybody!

—CEDRIC VONGERICHTEN

INTRODUCTION

Thai food, like all good comfort food, is full of love and perfect for sharing. Growing up in Thailand, my family connected the way every family does—over food, cooking and sharing meals, talking and tasting. That sense of connection is here on every page of this book, filling each recipe, and alongside tips on Thai ingredients and techniques, ideas for incorporating Thai flavors into your everyday cooking, and indispensible kitchen wisdom from the best cook in our family, Grandma Prapit.

The recipes and stories in this book come from our family kitchen in Chiang Mai, childhood vacations to visit my mother's family and the beaches of southern Thailand, the exciting years I worked in Bangkok, and dishes I love making today at Ngam, my restaurant in New York's East Village—family favorites, traditional regional classics, and even a few all-new recipes inspired by the particular flavors and memories of each place. For that reason, I've arranged the book by location, with four main chapters based on a significant place I've lived and where the recipes come from. At the end, you'll find useful recipes for staples including dipping sauces, curry pastes, and other delicious condiments or seasonings you can use every day, as well as an illustrated glossary of traditional Thai ingredients featured in the book.

We Thais are fiercely proud of our culture, so it's such a joy for me as a chef and food lover to share the flavors of true Thai cuisine with the world.

CHIANG MAI

Influenced by the cool, rainy climate of the lush mountain valleys as well as by traditions passed down from the ancient Isan and Lanna kingdoms of northeastern and northern Thailand, respectively, northern Thai cuisine has deep roots. Sticky rice takes the place of steamed rice and meals feature pungent dips and relishes, smoky grilled dishes, and aromatic curries made with giant river prawns, chicken, or pork. Travelers have turned my hometown, Chiang Mai, into a top world destination—it's both a center of traditional Thai culture and home to Chiang Mai University, and this combination of history and youthful energy keeps the city and its food richly exciting. These are the flavors I grew up with, including many family recipes and familiar dishes that always make me feel at home.

SOUTHERN THAILAND

Growing up, trips to the south meant long drives all the way to the beaches of Phuket to visit my mother's family. These times were always special and seemed like such a departure from daily life in Chiang Mai. Once for my birthday, a family friend took us by longboat to a preserved island surrounded by mangroves. We spent the day snorkeling in pristine waters and feasted that night on freshly caught seafood grilled right on the beach. The food of southern Thailand is like the place—bold, bright, and colorful. Here, the dishes are spicier, with sweet tropical fruit balancing the heat of red curry and chiles. The Gulf of Thailand to the west and the Indian Ocean to the east guarantee a near-constant variety of fresh seafood.

BANGKOK

Thailand's central plateau is a rich, flat, wet rice-growing region between the mountainous north and the tropical south that includes Bangkok. As a modern metropolis and an ancient center of royal power, the capital makes a great show of combining old and new, high and low, rich and poor, all on top of one another. Gleaming skyscrapers tower over temples and palaces; executives in sleek designer suits slurp bowls of noodles from street carts or in the floating markets. As a busy port, Bangkok is also where Thailand meets the world. Centuries of Chinese, Southeast Asian, and even Western influences have helped turn Bangkok into a glamorous cosmopolitan city where traditions and trends mingle deliciously. In Bangkok, I also had the great privilege of training with M. L. Sirichalerm Svasti, known as Chef McDang, one of the most celebrated Thai chefs in the world—what he taught me set me on the road to being a chef.

NEW YORK CITY

So far away from everything I knew, New York City is also the only place I could imagine all my dreams coming true. Here I found more mentors, including Ian Cerlermkittichai of Kittichai and Cedric and Jean-Georges Vongerichten at Spice Market and Perry St. They taught me so much about combining passion with craft to turn what you love into a real business and how to run a successful kitchen. New York City's unique energy, the crazy pace of living, and the sheer diversity of the faces, sounds, and flavors around every corner inspire me every day—it's a clash of cultures that forms new combinations out of familiar elements and outside influences.

True Thai is intended to share with you, at home, versions of the same dishes, flavors, and memories that I grew up with in Thailand and that I cook now for guests in my restaurant. There is love in every recipe and every story and I hope you find it there too.

—HONG THAIMEE

THAI MEALS

Thai cuisine celebrates a balance of strong, fundamental tastes—salty, sour, spicy, and sweet—achieving harmony with an intricate variety of different flavors, textures, and temperatures within a single dish and across the whole meal. Rice, *khao*, either as steamed rice or, more commonly in northern Thailand, sticky rice, is the centerpiece of a Thai meal, with a variety of highly flavored, complementary dishes served family style around it for all to share. As opposed to the timed courses of *antipasti*, *primi*, and *secondi* in a traditional Italian meal, in a traditional Thai meal all dishes are served together at once.

A good Thai host will want to offer one more dish than there are diners at the table, as well as a variety of cooking techniques within a meal, meaning a meal for four could include a highly flavored dip or relish for raw or cooked vegetables, a clear soup (such as a *tom yum*), a curry or stew, a deep-fried dish, and a stir-fried dish, each incorporating a combination of meat, seafood, and/or vegetables. This is why many of the recipes in this book can appear to serve a wide variety of diners: If offered family style with another dish or dishes and rice, most can serve four; if served as a stand-alone entrée, it may be better suited to a light meal for two, depending on appetite. In Thailand, fried rice and noodle dishes are commonly fast meals had on the go, but I've adjusted these recipes to fit into a meal.

Traditionally, Thais ate with their hands, often using a small pinch or handful of sticky rice as an implement to scoop up or dip into dishes. In the late nineteenth century, fearing colonial expansionism, King Rama V enacted broad cultural and social reforms, including introducing Western-style dining tables, chairs, and utensils. Today, most Thais eat with a fork and spoon, using the fork, held in the left hand, to push food onto the spoon, held in the right. Knives are typically not needed and chopsticks are used more or less exclusively for Chinese-style noodle soups (or at Chinese, Japanese, or Korean restaurants).

In Thailand, we cook with our hearts and trust to our *rod mue*—the flavor of your hand. That means that everyone knows his or her own palate best, so while following the recipes, all seasonings can be *rod mue*, or to taste. Similarly, any noodle dish can be prepared using your favorite style of noodle, simply adjust the cooking time—you can even omit the noodles entirely, which we call *gao lao*.

RECIPE INDEX

เชียงใหม่

CHIANG MAI

เชียงใหม่
CHIANG MAI

Banana Fritters
Gluay Khaek

Betel Bites
Miang Kham

Pork Satay
Moo Satay

Grandma's Sunny-Side-Up Eggs
Khai Daow Song Khrueng

Daddy's Egg Soup
Gaeng Jeut Khai Nam

Mom's Spicy Sour
Red Snapper Soup
Tom Yum Pla

Red Beet Broth Spectacular
Yen Tah Foh

Chiang Mai Raw Beef Salad
Saa Nua

Pomelo Salad
Yum Som Oh

Chiang Mai Egg Noodles
in Curry Broth
Khao Soy Gai

Noodles in *Tom Yum* Broth
Guay Tiew Tom Yum

Mom's Favorite Noodles
Guay Tiew Haeng

Noodles in Aromatic Beef Broth
Guay Tiew Nua Toon

Rice Noodles with Cherry
Tomatoes and Pork
(aka My Favorite Noodle Dish
in the Whole World)
Khanom Jeen Nam Ngiaw

Banana Blossom and
Shrimp Curry
Gaeng Lieng Hua Plee Gap Goong

Braised Pork Belly
in *Hung Lay* Curry
Gaeng Hung Lay

Stir-Fried Wild Boar
with Red Curry
Moo Ba Pad Phet

Ultimate Green Curry
with Chicken
Gaeng Khiaw Wan Gai

Braised Chicken Chiang
Mai–Style
Ook Gai

Chiang Mai Sausage
Sai Ooa

Chicken and Rice
Khao Mun Gai

Grilled Salt-Crusted Whole Fish
Pla Phao Glua

Lanna-Style Steamed Chicken
in Banana Leaves
Haw Nueng Gai

Midnight Fried Chicken
Gai Tod Tiang Kuen

Mom's Best Baby Back Ribs
See Klong Moo Tod

My Childhood Favorite: Eggs
and Pork Belly
Khai Palow

Northern Thai–Style Grilled
Fish in Banana Leaves
Ab Pla

Pork *Laab*
Laab Moo Chiang Mai

Red Fire Water Spinach
Pad Pak Boong Fai Daeng

Sautéed Sugar Snap Peas
with Oyster Sauce
Tua Lan Tao Pad Nam Mun Hoy

Coconut and Wild Sesame
Sticky Rice
Khao Nook Nga

Coconut Sticky Rice with Mango
Khao Niaw Mamuang

Jasmine Coconut Jelly
Woon Grati

Seasonal Fruit
with Candied Salted Chile
Pon La Mai Ruam Leh Prik
Gub Glua

กล้วยแขก

BANANA FRITTERS

GLUAY KHAEK

MAKES 12 TO 14 PIECES

These are total street food, a treat every kid in Thailand grows up with. Banana fritters were my after-school snack of choice, and I would routinely order a couple of pieces from the stall stationed in front of my school. Back then, they were served in recycled paper, and I mean truly recycled—often it was an old newspaper, which offered some light reading while snacking. The best part was the crispy batter made with coconut and sesame seeds. They always made the ride home a bit yummier.

1 pound sugar bananas or green plantains
   (see Note), peeled

1 cup rice flour

½ cup unsweetened dried coconut

2 tablespoons sugar

1 tablespoon white sesame seeds

1½ teaspoons baking soda

Pinch of salt

½ cup water

2 quarts vegetable oil

Slice the bananas lengthwise ¼ inch thick and set aside.

In a medium bowl, combine the rice flour, dried coconut, sugar, sesame seeds, baking soda, salt, and water until well blended.

Pour the oil into a large high-sided skillet or heavy-bottomed saucepan, place over high heat, and heat to 350°F. Dip one banana slice into the batter to lightly coat it on all sides and, very carefully, gently slide it into the hot oil. Quickly batter a few more banana slices and add them to the oil, being careful not to crowd the pan, and fry until golden brown, about 5 minutes, turning the slices a few times.

Using a slotted spoon, transfer to a tray lined with paper towels to drain excess oil and repeat battering and frying the remaining banana slices. Serve immediately.

NOTE: Sugar bananas, also known as Lady Finger bananas, are shorter, thinner-skinned, and somewhat

sweeter than common bananas. The national fruit of Cambodia, they're common in Southeast Asia, but aren't hard to find in Asian or even Latin American fruit markets, where they might be called bocadillos. I personally prefer firmer, starchier bananas over softer or overripe ones, since they hold up better in this recipe, making green plantains a fine substitute.

BETEL BITES

MIANG KHAM

MAKES 20 BETEL BITES

A very traditional, old-school Thai snack, this was my grandmother's favorite. Not only are betel leaves (*bai cha plu*) packed with medicinal power, but the varied condiments I serve them with add tons of flavor—fragrant jam, sweet but sharp ginger, salty dried shrimp, crunchy coconut and peanuts, a splash of tanginess from lime, and spicy Thai chile. Each bite will taste slightly different from the next. The best part is you can pick and choose your own flavor adventure!

FOR THE MIANG JAM

1 cup shaved palm sugar

1 cup fish sauce

1 tablespoon shrimp paste, or to taste

1 tablespoon finely chopped galangal

1 tablespoon finely chopped lemongrass

2 tablespoons dried shrimp, finely ground using a mortar and pestle or in a mini food processor (optional)

FOR ASSEMBLY

20 betel leaves (see Note), washed and dried

½ cup peanuts, toasted

1 lime, including rind, finely diced

½ cup toasted unsweetened dried coconut flakes

1 to 2 fresh red Thai chiles, sliced into very thin rounds

1 (1-inch) piece ginger, finely diced

1 to 2 shallots, diced

1 to 2 tablespoons dried shrimp

TO MAKE THE MIANG JAM: In a medium saucepan, combine the palm sugar, fish sauce, and shrimp paste, place over medium heat, and bring to a boil. Boil, stirring, until the sugar and shrimp paste have dissolved, then add the galangal, lemongrass, and dried shrimp and cook until the mixture is reduced to the consistency of a jam, about 5 minutes. Remove from the pan to a bowl to cool.

TO ASSEMBLE: Arrange the betel leaves, peanuts, diced lime, dried coconut, chile rounds, and diced ginger and shallots on a large plate. To eat, take a betel leaf, fill it with the ingredients of your choice, top with some Miang jam, fold into a bite-size package, and pop it into your mouth.

NOTE: If you can't find betel leaves near you in Asian markets, you can buy them online (grown in Florida), or substitute radicchio, endive, or even romaine lettuce leaves. Each offers a different flavor, but the idea of the Miang, a bright fresh snack bursting with many flavors in small bites, will still be there.

หมูสะเต๊ะ

PORK SATAY

MOO SATAY

SERVES 4

Satay refers to grilling thin strips of marinated meat over coals. Here I marinate thinly sliced pork tenderloin with coconut milk and a variety of seasonings, and when it hits the grill, the *satay* aroma is oh-so inviting. This recipe would also work with chicken, beef, or shrimp.

2 stalks lemongrass, finely chopped

1 (1-inch) piece galangal, finely chopped

2 teaspoons cumin seeds, toasted and ground

2 teaspoons coriander seeds, toasted and ground

1 small knob fresh turmeric, finely chopped,
    or 2 teaspoons ground turmeric

2 tablespoons fish sauce

1 cup coconut milk

2 pounds pork tenderloin, thinly sliced

8 ounces pork fat, cut into ½ × ½-inch pieces
    (optional)

40 wooden skewers, soaked 30 minutes to 1 hour
    in water (to prevent burning on the grill)

Cucumber Relish (page 226)

Peanut Sauce (recipe follows)

In a large bowl, whisk together the lemongrass, galangal, cumin, coriander, turmeric, fish sauce, and coconut milk until well blended. Add the pork and marinate on the counter for 45 minutes, or preferably overnight in the refrigerator.

Heat a charcoal grill to medium heat. Thread the meat and pieces of pork fat down the length of the skewer, keeping the meat as flat and flush with the skewer as possible for grilling, leaving 2 to 3 inches free to use as a handle. Set aside.

Grill the pork skewers for 3 to 4 minutes on each side, until cooked through. Serve with Cucumber Relish and Peanut Sauce.

PEANUT SAUCE

MAKES 3 CUPS

2 cups coconut milk

½ cup Red Curry Paste (page 229)

1 cup peanuts, coarsely chopped

¼ cup palm sugar

¼ cup tamarind concentrate

2 tablespoons fish sauce

In a small saucepan, combine 2 tablespoons of the coconut milk with the red curry paste. Place over medium heat and stir until the paste is dissolved and the mixture is aromatic, about 2 minutes. Add the peanuts and the remaining coconut milk. Cook, stirring, for 4 to 5 minutes, until slightly thickened. Add the sugar, tamarind concentrate, and fish sauce, raise the heat to medium-high, and simmer for about 5 minutes.

TIPS: Since you only chop the light-colored bottom 2 to 3 inches from the root of each stalk of lemongrass, you can bruise the remaining woody stalk and turn it into an aromatic basting brush. Carefully bash the cut end of the stalk with the back or flat side of your knife or a kitchen mallet till bruised and pliant. Dip the bruised end into the coconut milk mixture and brush the satays for the first minute they're on the grill. This will make them even more fragrant and tender.

ไข่ดาวทรงเครื่อง

GRANDMA'S SUNNY-SIDE-UP EGGS

KHAI DAOW SONG KHRUENG

SERVES 1

Grandma Prapit is the best cook I have ever met. She can make a great dish out of anything. When she decided to leave my grandpa, she moved her nine kids to Bangkok and started a new life with nothing but her cooking skills. She lived with us for as long as I remember. Back then, she made this recipe with crispy pork, but I have taken the liberty of using bacon instead. I am sure she is smiling at me from above, happy to see me continue the tradition, even if slightly updated. After all, ultimately it is love that makes the dish.

2 strips bacon

2 large eggs

Hot steamed jasmine or brown rice

2 teaspoons Simple Thai Salad Dressing (page 237)

1 to 2 fresh red Thai chiles, sliced

1 very small clove garlic, or to taste, thinly sliced

1 teaspoon thinly sliced shallot

Cilantro leaves

In a skillet, fry the bacon until crisp, then drain and crumble (you can also dice the bacon before frying). In a separate skillet, fry the eggs sunny-side-up till the edges are crisp but the yolks remain runny, or to your liking.

Spoon some rice onto a plate and top with the fried eggs and crumbled bacon.

Season to taste with the salad dressing, sliced chiles, garlic, shallot, and cilantro.

แกงจืดไข่น้ำ

DADDY'S EGG SOUP

GAENG JEUT KHAI NAM

SERVES 4

My dad doesn't cook much, but when he does, he can turn something ordinary into something special. Just like Grandma, he taught me to not be afraid of being creative in the kitchen, and this soup is a great example of his type of kitchen magic. All you need is a simple broth, farm-fresh eggs, and some aromatic scallions and cilantro. Who can say no to that?

6 cups Thai Chicken Stock (page 236)

8 ounces ground pork

1 teaspoon finely chopped cilantro root

1 teaspoon finely chopped garlic

½ teaspoon ground white pepper

1 tablespoon oyster sauce

**4 large farm-fresh eggs
(the fresher the better), beaten**

1 cup very roughly chopped cilantro

2 scallions, cut into 2-inch pieces

1 tablespoon mushroom sauce, or to taste

In a large saucepan, bring the stock to a boil over high heat.

Meanwhile, in a medium bowl, mix the ground pork, cilantro root, garlic, white pepper, and oyster sauce with your hands until the ingredients are well incorporated. Roll into 1-inch balls and place on a plate.

Add the meatballs to the boiling stock and cook for about 5 minutes, skimming foam from the top as needed, until the meatballs float and are fully cooked. Lower the heat to maintain a simmer.

Pour the beaten eggs in a circle along the inner edge of the pan. The eggs will cook almost instantly and it will look like a cloud of eggs in the soup. Add the cilantro and scallions and add the mushroom sauce. Remove from the heat and spoon into bowls.

ต้มยำปลา

MOM'S SPICY SOUR RED SNAPPER SOUP

TOM YUM PLA

SERVES 4

This dish is my mom's claim to fame. When she makes it, my job is to help her squeeze the limes, pick the chiles, bruise the lemongrass, tear the kaffir lime leaves, slice the galangal, and wash the cilantro. My hard work pays off by the end of the meal when the bowl is inevitably left empty. For a delicious vegetarian version, use vegetable stock and substitute mushrooms and mushroom sauce for the fish and fish sauce.

6 cups Thai Chicken Stock (page 236)

3 stalks lemongrass, cut into 3-inch pieces and bruised

5 kaffir lime leaves, torn into quarters

¼ cup sliced galangal (¼- to ½-inch coins)

3 small shallots, peeled and bruised

1 pound red snapper fillets, cut into bite-size pieces

3 ounces oyster mushrooms (about 1 cup)

1 to 4 fresh red Thai chiles, bruised, or to taste

¼ cup fish sauce, or to taste

¼ cup lime juice, or to taste

¼ cup coarsely chopped culantro (some reserved for garnish)

¼ cup coarsely chopped cilantro (some reserved for garnish)

In a large saucepan, bring the stock to a boil. Lower the heat to maintain a simmer and add the lemongrass, kaffir lime leaves, galangal, and shallots. Add the snapper and mushrooms and simmer until the snapper is opaque and has firmed up a little, about 5 minutes.

Remove from the heat and add the chiles, fish sauce, lime juice, culantro, and cilantro. Ladle into bowls and serve garnished with the remaining culantro and cilantro.

NOTE: Always add lime juice off the heat. Adding it to boiling water or soup will turn it bitter.

เย็นตาโฟ

RED BEET BROTH SPECTACULAR

YEN TAH FOH

SERVES 4

When I was growing up, the best place to get this dish was right across the street from the movie theater, and my dad would take us there often. The restaurant moved close to Chiang Mai University just before I started studying there, so I still got to eat it as a college student! The location change didn't affect the food or the atmosphere, from the rich flavor of the broth to the shade of red lipstick on the woman who makes the noodles. Here I've created a dish that uses the deep flavors of the original broth as a backdrop for one of my favorite ingredients, red beets—a variation on the original that still satisfies my Thai soul.

2 quarts Thai Chicken Stock (page 236)

1 medium Japanese radish, peeled and cut into 1-inch cubes (about 2 cups)

2 quarts vegetable oil

4 whole wonton skins

1 (12-ounce) package firm tofu, cut into 1-inch cubes

1 pound your choice of noodles (about 4 ounces per serving): flat rice noodles (*sen yai*), rice stick noodles (*sen lek*), vermicelli noodles (*woonsen*), egg noodles (*sen mee lung*) (or you can make it without noodles)

1 pound large shrimp (about 2 per serving)

4 ounces cleaned and sliced calamari

8 fish balls or shrimp balls

Yen Tah Foh Sauce (recipe follows)

Four classic Thai condiments (page 225)

In a large saucepan, combine the stock and Japanese radish. Place over medium-high heat and bring just to a boil. Reduce the heat and simmer for about 30 minutes, until the broth is slightly reduced. Keep hot.

In a large saucepan, heat the oil over medium-high heat until it reaches 375°F. Add the wonton skins and fry until golden brown on all sides, turning them with tongs, 2 to 3 minutes. Using tongs, transfer to a baking sheet lined with paper towels. Let the oil return to 375°F, add the tofu, and fry until golden brown on all sides, about 5 minutes. Using a slotted spoon, transfer to the paper towel–lined baking sheet.

Ready four individual soup bowls. In a large saucepan, bring 3 quarts water to a boil over high heat, and set the pan up with a blanching basket or steamer insert. Blanch the noodles for 3 to 5 minutes, until tender, then divide among soup bowls. Repeat with the shrimp, calamari, and fish or shrimp balls, until the meat is fully cooked, about 3 minutes. Divide the blanched seafood amongß the soup bowls, then top each with 2 tablespoons Yen Tah Foh Sauce.

Ladle in the hot broth along with the radish, adding enough broth to cover the noodles. Top with the fried wontons and tofu and serve with the four classic Thai condiments.

YEN TAH FOH SAUCE

Red fermented bean curd is a popular condiment in Thai cuisine often used to flavor rice and porridge dishes. It's a thick paste with a flavor both salty and mildly sweet. The addition of fermented red yeast rice gives the paste its distinctive color as well as a richer aroma and flavor.

1 tablespoon salt

1 cup chopped red beets (4 to 6 beets, halved if small, quartered if large)

½ cup red fermented bean curd

2 to 3 fresh Thai red chiles

½ cup lime juice

½ cup fish sauce

½ cup sugar

Bring a large saucepan of water to a boil over high heat and prepare an ice bath. Add the salt and chopped beets to the boiling water and blanch until the beets are tender, 8 to 10 minutes. Immediately transfer to the ice bath to cool, then drain.

Combine the beets with the remaining ingredients in a blender and blend until well combined.

ส้าเนื้อ

CHIANG MAI RAW BEEF SALAD

SAA NUA

SERVES 2 TO 4

When I decided to pursue a career in cooking, I had the opportunity to work as a kitchen intern at Le Grand Lanna at the Mandarin Oriental Dhara Dhevi, now the Dhara Dhevi Chiang Mai. Not only was it a fun experience, but I learned so much from the seasoned cooks there. One of them was Mae Aong, a petite lady who is a foremost expert on northern Thai food—I call her my personal Wikipedia on Chiang Mai cooking techniques. One day she made me this traditional beef dish; with my first bite, I was hooked. *Saa* is prepared in the same style as *laab* (page 82), but with *laab* the meat is chopped and ground rather than sliced into strips.

In this light preparation I leave the beef raw. As with any raw beef dish, such as a carpaccio or tartare, care should be taken to select only the best, most reliable sources for the beef and to keep the meat at the proper temperature (below 40°F) until you're ready to serve.

8 ounces beef tenderloin, chilled and thinly sliced against the grain

1 small shallot, thinly sliced

2 cloves garlic, minced

1 stalk lemongrass, thinly sliced

3 to 4 kaffir lime leaves, cut into thin chiffonade

2 tablespoons thinly sliced mint

2 tablespoons thinly sliced Vietnamese mint

2 tablespoons thinly sliced culantro

5 sprigs cilantro, finely chopped

1 scallion, thinly sliced

1 tablespoon fish sauce

1 tablespoon *laab* chile (page 83), or to taste

In a large bowl, combine all of the ingredients. Transfer to a plate and serve.

NOTE: To make a cooked version of the dish: Heat a small amount of oil in a large skillet or wok and briefly cook the shallot and garlic to soften. Add the beef and toss till lightly browned, then add the lemongrass, scallion, fish sauce, and *laab* chile and stir-fry to the desired doneness. Off the heat, toss with the lime leaves, mint, culantro, and cilantro.

ยำส้มโอ

POMELO SALAD

YUM SOM OH

SERVES 4

Pomelo is similar to grapefruit, but larger and sweeter. The peel is thicker, soft but dense with the sweet aroma of a citrus fruit. A pomelo section is lumpy, and though the membrane is dry, the segments are packed with juice. Thai varieties usually have light yellow-white flesh, while pale pink to almost ruby red is more common here. They are delicious on their own, but when combined with the fresh aromas of kaffir lime leaves and lemongrass and the smoky crunch of toasted coconut, the flavor and textural sensations of this salad are like a party in your mouth!

FOR THE DRESSING

4 dried red Thai chiles

2 tablespoons coarsely chopped shallot

2 tablespoons chopped garlic

¼ cup fish sauce (substitute mushroom sauce if vegetarian)

¼ cup palm sugar

¼ cup tamarind concentrate

FOR THE SALAD

½ cup vegetable oil

2 small shallots, thinly sliced into rounds

1 pomelo, peeled, segmented, and cut into 1-inch pieces

½ cup unsweetened coconut flakes, toasted

½ cup coarsely chopped peanuts

4 kaffir lime leaves, cut into thin chiffonade, plus extra (optional) for garnish

2 stalks lemongrass, thinly sliced

TO MAKE THE DRESSING: Place the chiles in a bowl and add warm water to cover. Leave to soften for about 15 minutes. Wearing kitchen gloves (do not use bare hands when working with chiles), remove the chiles from the water and squeeze out excess water.

In a stone mortar, combine the chiles, shallot, and garlic and pound with a pestle into a smooth paste. Set aside.

In a medium saucepan, combine the fish sauce, sugar, and tamarind concentrate. Place over medium heat and heat, stirring, until the sugar is dissolved. Add the chile paste and stir to combine. Reduce the heat to low and cook until the sauce thickens enough to coat the back of a spoon, about 10 minutes. Transfer to a bowl and set aside to cool.

TO MAKE THE SALAD: In a small skillet, heat the oil over low heat until just shimmering. Add the shallots and fry until golden brown and crisp. Drain on a paper towel–lined plate and set aside.

In a medium bowl, combine the pomelo, coconut flakes, peanuts, fried shallots, kaffir lime leaves, and lemongrass and toss with the dressing and until well coated. Serve, garnished with additional kaffir lime leaves if you like.

NOTES: If you are looking for a substitute for peanuts, use cashews or increase the amount of coconut flakes.

ข้าวซอยไก่

CHIANG MAI EGG NOODLES IN CURRY BROTH

KHAO SOY GAI

SERVES 4 TO 6

This is one of Chiang Mai's most famous dishes. The combination of flavors and textures—creamy curry sauce and silky egg noodles married with the flavorful crunch of pickled mustard and crispy fried noodles, all given an awakening hit of fresh, zingy lime—is magical. Black cardamom pods are roasted over a wood fire to give them incredible smoky flavor.

FOR THE *KHAO SOY* PASTE

2 to 3 shallots, peeled

1 (2-inch) piece ginger, peeled

7 dried long red Thai chiles

1 teaspoon salt

1 ½ teaspoons coriander seeds, toasted

2 black cardamom pods, toasted

1 tablespoon chopped fresh turmeric

FOR THE CHILE OIL

2 tablespoons vegetable oil

2 tablespoons red Thai chile powder

½ teaspoon salt

FOR THE SOUP

6 cups fresh egg noodles

3 tablespoons plus 1 quart vegetable oil

4 (13.5-ounce) cans coconut milk

4 chicken thighs

½ cup fish sauce

½ cup palm sugar

For serving: pickled mustard, lime wedges, thinly sliced shallots

TO MAKE THE *KHAO SOY* PASTE: Preheat the oven to 400°F. Wrap the shallots and ginger together in aluminum foil, place directly on an oven rack, and roast for 10 minutes, or until softened. Remove from the foil and cool completely.

Meanwhile, place the dried chiles in a bowl and add warm water to cover. Leave to soften for about 15 minutes. Wearing kitchen gloves (do not use bare hands when working with chiles), remove the chiles from the water and squeeze out excess water.

Using a mortar and pestle, mash the chiles with the shallots, ginger, salt, coriander, cardamom, and turmeric into a smooth paste, about 15 minutes. Alternatively, process the ingredients together with 1 cup coconut milk in a food processor until smooth, 3 to 5 minutes.

TO MAKE THE CHILE OIL: In a small skillet, combine the oil and chile powder over medium heat until well blended. Add the salt and cook, stirring, until the salt dissolves, about 2 minutes. Transfer to a bowl and set aside.

TO MAKE THE SOUP: Place the noodles on a large baking sheet pan and pull them apart so they don't stick together in the pot. Divide the noodles into a 4-cup portion and a 2-cup portion.

In a large pot, bring 3 quarts water to a boil over high heat. Add 4 cups of the noodles and cook until softened, about 4 minutes. Drain the noodles and rinse with cold water. Set aside. Toss with the 3 tablespoons vegetable oil to keep the noodles from sticking.

Skim 2 tablespoons coconut cream from the top of one of the cans of coconut milk and set aside. In a medium saucepan, combine the *kao soy* paste with the 2 tablespoons coconut cream, place over medium heat, and cook until the color intensifies, about 3 minutes.

Add the chicken skin side down and cook until the skin browns, about 3 minutes. Add the remaining coconut milk and bring just to a boil. Reduce the heat to low and add the fish sauce and sugar. Simmer for another 15 minutes, stirring to dissolve the sugar, until the chicken is cooked and the sauce thickens.

As the chicken cooks, with the remaining 2 cups noodles, use your hands to form four ½-cup-size nests. Pour the remaining 1 quart vegetable oil into a large pot or wide sauté pan deep enough for the oil to cover the noodles. Place over high heat and bring to 375°F. Add the nests of noodles and fry over high heat until golden and crisp, 3 to 4 minutes. Using a slotted spoon, transfer to a paper towel–lined baking sheet to drain the excess oil.

TO SERVE: Spoon some boiled noodles into each of four bowls, top with a ladle of curry and a piece of chicken, and finish with a nest of fried noodles. Serve with chile oil, pickled mustard, lime wedges, and thinly sliced shallots.

ก๋วยเตี๋ยวต้มยำ

NOODLES IN *TOM YUM* BROTH

GUAY TIEW TOM YUM

SERVES 4

Guay tiew is Thai cuisine's version of *pho*. We have it for breakfast, lunch, dinner, even late at night. You can find it at *tor roong* (strolling the night market), streetside stalls, or fancy restaurants; wherever I eat it, I feel at home. The quality of *guay tiew* is judged by the broth: Here my Pork Stock flavored with daikon and cilantro root adds a natural sweetness, and the seasoning offers elements of spicy and sour.

2 quarts vegetable oil

8 wonton wrappers

2 quarts Pork Stock (page 236)

1 teaspoon red Thai chile powder, or to taste

2 teaspoons lime juice, or to taste

2 teaspoons fish sauce, or to taste

1 teaspoon sugar, or to taste

1 pound ground pork (optional: mix in
    2 tablespoons mushroom sauce, or to taste)

Pork offal (such as heart or liver), thinly sliced
    (optional)

4 to 8 fish balls (1 to 2 per person)

1 pound *sen yai* flat rice noodles

2 cups bean sprouts

4 teaspoons Fried Garlic (page 231)

1 cup toasted peanuts

1 sprig cilantro, finely chopped

1 scallion, finely chopped

Pinch of freshly ground white pepper

Line a baking sheet with paper towels. In a large saucepan, heat the oil to 375°F. Drop in the wonton wrappers one at a time and fry in batches, being careful not to crowd the pan, until golden and crisp, 3 to 4 minutes. Using tongs or a slotted spoon, transfer to the prepared baking sheet to drain excess oil.

In another large saucepan, bring the stock just to a simmer over medium heat, then lower the heat and cover to keep the stock hot. In a separate medium saucepan, bring 3 quarts water to a boil and set the pan up with a blanching basket or steamer insert. Divide the red Thai chile powder, lime juice, fish sauce, and sugar among four individual serving bowls, then add 1/4 cup hot pork stock to each bowl to mix.

Blanch the pork offal, if using, or fish balls in the boiling water just until no longer pink and the fish balls are hot, 3 to 5 minutes, and divide among the serving bowls with a slotted spoon. Blanch the ground pork for about 5 minutes, until cooked through and no longer pink, and divide among the serving bowls. Blanch the noodles for about 2 minutes, then add the bean sprouts and cook for 1 to 2 more minutes, until the noodles are tender and bean sprouts are wilted. Divide these among the bowls then top with the remaining hot pork stock. Season each bowl with the fried garlic, cilantro, scallion, and white pepper.

ก๋วยเตี๋ยวแห้ง

MOM'S FAVORITE NOODLES

GUAY TIEW HAENG

SERVES 4

My mom prefers her noodle soup without the soup. To make it, all you have to do is cook the noodles and add the rest of the ingredients. In some ways, it's more like a noodle salad. It's definitely a faster way of making noodle soup!

1 pound pork tenderloin, thinly sliced

1 pound pork balls (optional)

Pork offal, such as heart or liver, thinly sliced (optional)

1 pound *sen lek* rice stick noodles

Fried Garlic (page 231) with 1 tablespoon of the garlic oil

FOR TOPPING

Black soy sauce

½ cup ground peanuts

2 cups bean sprouts

1 lime, cut into 4 wedges

Red Thai chile powder

4 fried wonton skins (see page 33)

1 sprig cilantro, finely chopped

1 scallion, finely chopped

2 teaspoons freshly ground white pepper

Classic four Thai condiments (page 225)

In a large saucepan, bring 2 quarts water to a boil. Add the pork tenderloin, pork balls, and pork offal, if using, and blanch for about 3 minutes, then add the noodles and blanch together for another 2 to 3 minutes, until the noodles are soft and the pork no longer pink. Drain and transfer to a large bowl. Toss with the garlic oil to prevent the noodles from sticking.

Divide the noodles among four bowls, season with black soy sauce (1 to 2 teaspoons per bowl), and add the ground peanuts, bean sprouts, lime wedges, chile to taste, and wonton skins. Top each bowl with cilantro, scallion, and ½ teaspoon white pepper. Serve with the classic four Thai condiments.

ก๋วยเตี๋ยวเนื้อตุ๋น

NOODLES IN AROMATIC BEEF BROTH

GUAY TIEW NUA TOON

SERVES 4

This beef noodle dish has a savory, rejuvenating power. As a firm believer that *Kong tup tong dern duay tong*, or "An army runs on its stomach," I knew that if my book's photography team were well fed, the quality of our work would be better. So, after we got off the flight from New York City to Chiang Mai to shoot this cookbook, I took the crew straight to my favorite beef noodle place on Chang Klan Road, not far from the airport. My strategy worked! The bewilderment and fatigue of jetlag faded away with every sip of the cinnamon-scented broth, and we got in a full day of shooting.

1 pound clear vermicelli

2 pounds beef short ribs

10 cilantro roots, cleaned

10 cloves garlic, bruised

2 tablespoons whole black peppercorns

1 (3-inch) piece galangal

2 pieces star anise

2 cinnamon sticks

7 pieces black cardamom

2 bay leaves

¼ cup light brown sugar, or to taste

½ cup mushroom sauce, or to taste

½ cup light soy sauce, or to taste

8 ounces bean sprouts

8 ounces water spinach

Beef offal, such as heart or liver, sliced (optional)

Beef balls (optional)

Fried Garlic (page 231)

½ cup finely diced Chinese celery

Classic four Thai condiments (page 225)

Hydrate the vermicelli noodles in a large bowl or pan of room temperature water just till soft, about 20 minutes. If long, cut the noodles into 8- to 10-inch lengths.

In a medium saucepan, bring 6 quarts water to a boil over high heat. Add the short ribs, cilantro roots, garlic, peppercorns, galangal, star anise, cinnamon sticks, cardamom, bay leaves, brown sugar, mushroom sauce, and soy sauce. Lower the heat to maintain a low simmer and braise for about 3 hours, until the beef is tender, skimming the foam off the top as necessary to keep the broth clear. Set the braised ribs aside and keep the broth hot.

In a second saucepan, bring 3 quarts water to a boil and set the pan up with a blanching basket or steamer insert. Ready four individual serving bowls. Blanch the offal and beef balls, if using, just till no longer pink, 3 to 5 minutes, then remove to a bowl with a slotted spoon. Add the noodles to the boiling water and blanch just until tender, about 2 minutes, then add the bean sprouts and water spinach just until wilted, another 1 to 2 minutes. Divide the noodles, bean sprouts, and water spinach among the serving bowls and discard the blanching liquid. Divide the braised beef, offal, and beef ball, if using, among the bowls.

Top each bowl with the hot broth and garnish with fried garlic and the Chinese celery. Serve with the classic four Thai condiments.

ขนมจีนน้ำเงี้ยว

RICE NOODLES WITH CHERRY TOMATOES AND PORK

(aka My Favorite Noodle Dish in the Whole World)

KHANOM JEEN NAM NGIAW

SERVES 4 TO 6

Nam ngiaw captures everything you want in a dish: It's aromatic from the chile paste, sweet from the pork, and sour from the cherry tomatoes. Bean sprouts, pickled mustard greens, and a squeeze of lime bring a splash of freshness, and fried garlic, chiles, and crispy pork rinds add satisfying crunch. Cook this delicious dish in a big pot so the whole family can enjoy it together.

Though *khanom jeen* can be found fresh in the market in Thailand, here, these soft rice noodles are usually dried—*somen* noodles, available in Japanese markets, will have a similar texture. Dried *ngiaw* flowers are also known as cotton tree flowers and can be found at Thai markets or online.

2 pounds baby back ribs

10 dried *ngiaw* flowers (optional)

10 dried long red Thai chiles

10 cilantro roots, cleaned (or 2 whole bunches cilantro)

½ cup peeled cloves garlic

½ shallot, peeled

3 tablespoons shrimp paste

½ cup vegetable oil

1 pound ground pork

½ cup Thai miso

10 ounces *khanom jeen* soft rice vermicelli noodles

3 cubes chicken or pork blood (see Note)

1 cup cherry tomatoes, cut in half

3 tablespoons fish sauce, or to taste

Condiments: Fried Garlic (page 231), finely chopped cilantro, finely chopped scallions, crispy dried Thai chiles, lime wedges, bean sprouts, finely chopped pickled mustard, crispy pork rinds

In a medium pot, bring 2 quarts water to a boil over high heat. Lower the heat to medium, add the ribs, and cook for about 1 hour, until the meat is tender. Set aside in the liquid.

If using the dried *ngiaw* flowers, place them in a bowl and add warm water to cover. Leave to soften for 15 minutes, then drain and set aside.

Meanwhile, place the dried chiles in a second bowl and add warm water to cover. Leave to soften for about 15 minutes. Wearing kitchen gloves (do not use bare hands when working with chiles), remove the chiles from the water and squeeze out excess water.

In a stone mortar, combine the hydrated chiles, the cilantro roots, garlic, and shallot and pound with a pestle until it forms a coarse paste, about 15 minutes. Add the shrimp paste and mix well. Set aside.

In a wok or a large sauté pan, heat the oil over medium heat. Add the chile paste and cook, stirring, until fragrant, about 2 minutes. Add the ground pork and Thai miso and cook, stirring, until the pork and paste are well combined and the meat is cooked through, about 5 minutes.

Meanwhile, bring 3 quarts water a boil in a medium pot. Add the noodles and cook for 8 to 10 minutes, until tender. Remove the cooked noodles and immediately rinse under cold water, then set aside.

Add the ground pork mixture to the pot with the ribs. Add the rehydrated *ngiaw* flowers, if using, and simmer for another 15 minutes, until the ground pork is cooked and the broth slightly reduced. Add the blood cubes and cherry tomatoes and simmer for another 5 to 10 minutes, until the flavors are well incorporated and the tomatoes just softened. Divide the noodles among serving bowls, spoon the soup on top, and serve with traditional condiments.

NOTE: Cubed pork blood and chicken blood are common ingredients in northern Thai cuisine, where they add deep, savory flavor to curries and stews. If unavailable or unappealing, you can substitute chopped chicken livers for a similar effect.

แกงเลียงหัวปลีกับกุ้ง

BANANA BLOSSOM AND SHRIMP CURRY

GAENG LIENG HUA PLEE GAP GOONG

SERVES 4

I remember the day I first tried this curry in our elementary school's home economics class—we got to wear aprons and actually learn how to cook! I can still hear the sound of the stone mortar and smell the aroma of the curry paste filling my classroom as if it were yesterday. I remember thinking, *Wow! Cooking isn't hard, and it's super fun!*

Finding fresh banana blossoms may prove challenging; your best bet is to look in summer in Asian—especially Filipino, Thai, or Vietnamese—markets. Recipe-ready canned banana blossoms can be used in a pinch.

FOR THE CURRY PASTE

3 ounces medium shrimp, peeled, deveined, and tails removed

2 pieces krachai

½ cup coarsely chopped shallots

1½ teaspoons whole black peppercorns

2 teaspoons shrimp paste

FOR THE CURRY

4 cups Thai Chicken Stock (page 236)

1 medium banana blossom, prepared (see page 52)

1 cup cubed pumpkin or winter squash such as butternut or delicata (1-inch cubes)

1 cup chopped king oyster mushrooms (3 to 4 ounces)

4 ounces medium shrimp, peeled, deveined, and tails removed

½ cup whole lemon basil leaves

2 teaspoons fish sauce, or to taste

Steamed jasmine or brown rice

TO MAKE THE CURRY PASTE: First, fill a bowl with ice and water to make an ice bath and set aside.

Bring a medium pot of water to a boil over high heat. Add the shrimp and cook until pink, 1 to 2 minutes. Using a slotted spoon, transfer to the ice bath to cool for 1 to 2 minutes. Drain the shrimp and squeeze them to remove excess liquid (to prevent the paste from becoming watery). Transfer to a stone mortar or a food processor, add the krachai, shallots, peppercorns, and shrimp paste, and pound for about 5 minutes in the mortar or process for about 2 minutes in the food processor, scraping the sides of the machine once or twice, until it forms a coarse paste. Set aside.

TO MAKE THE CURRY: Pour the stock into a medium saucepan, place over high heat, and bring to a boil. Add the curry paste, banana blossom, cubed pumpkin, and mushrooms. Lower the heat to maintain a simmer and cook until the banana blossom and pumpkin soften and the colors intensify, 8 to 10 minutes.

Add the shrimp and cook just until pink, 1 to 2 minutes; watch closely, as this can happen fast. Remove from the heat, stir in the lemon basil, and season with the fish sauce. Serve over steamed jasmine or brown rice.

How to Prepare Banana Blossoms

Banana blossoms contain a sap that will stick to your knife and cutting board and, like artichoke hearts, they quickly discolor when exposed to the air. To protect both your tools and the blossom itself, fill a large bowl with water and squeeze in a juicy lime half. Run the other half along the edge of a sharp knife and over your cutting board, then toss it into the bowl of water.

Peel off the dark, rough outer leaves of the blossom to reveal the lighter pink and white interior. Quarter the peeled blossom lengthwise, then slice out the center core and any baby buds inside.

Slice the cored quarters crosswise into 1-inch or bite-size pieces. Keep the slices in the lime water until ready to use, then drain.

แกงฮังเล

BRAISED PORK BELLY IN *HUNG LAY* CURRY

GAENG HUNG LAY

SERVES 4

Legend has it that *hung lay* became the signature dish of northern Thailand during the long years of war with Burma, now Myanmar. Growing up, it was on the menu of every holiday feast: at *khantoke* dinner (see photo), housewarming parties, weddings, traditional celebrations, even funerals. As the dish is rich in both history and flavor, there is no question why this has become one of the most famous of all northern Thai dishes.

I like to think of my version of *hung lay* as a modern-day "pot-of-love." I make my own curry paste, and use *hung lay* powder from a spice stand at Waroros Market in the heart of Chiang Mai (you can find it in Indian and Thai markets and online, or substitute with masala curry powder from a good spice market). While I'm braising it in my pressure cooker, I can imagine my dad exclaiming in his northern Thai dialect, "Mee hung lay toey . . . mor kanard!" ("Oh, there is *hung lay* . . . delectable!"). And when the smell of the curry fills the house, it's nothing but love all around!

FOR THE *HUNG LAY* CURRY PASTE

5 dried long red Thai chiles

Salt

¼ cup coarsely chopped shallots

¼ cup coarsely chopped garlic

2 tablespoons coarsely chopped lemongrass

1 tablespoon coarsely chopped galangal

1½ tablespoons shrimp paste

FOR THE PORK

1 pound pork neck, cut into 2-inch cubes

1 pound pork belly, cut into 2-inch cubes

2 tablespoons *hung lay* powder

2 tablespoons vegetable oil

3 cups water

½ cup palm sugar

½ cup tamarind concentrate

½ cup julienned ginger

½ cup pickled garlic

½ cup fish sauce

¼ cup black soy sauce

MAKE THE *HUNG LAY* CURRY PASTE:
Place the dried chiles in a bowl and add warm water to cover. Leave to soften for about 15 minutes. Wearing kitchen gloves (do not use bare hands when working with chiles), remove the chiles from the water and squeeze out excess water.

Using a mortar and pestle, mash the chiles with a generous pinch of salt (this keeps it from splattering). Add the shallots, garlic, lemongrass, galangal, and shrimp paste and mash until well blended into a paste, 10 to 15 minutes. Alternatively, process the ingredients in a food processor with a little vegetable oil for 3 minutes, or until smooth.

MAKE THE PORK: In a large bowl, toss the pork neck and pork belly with the curry paste and *hung lay* powder. Cover with plastic wrap and refrigerate for at least 1 hour or up to overnight; the longer you marinate it, the deeper and richer the flavor will be.

Heat the oil in a pressure cooker over medium-high heat. Add the pork and cook until it starts to brown on both sides and the aroma of the curry paste and powder have intensified, about 5 minutes.

Gently pour in the water and stir to deglaze the pan. Add the sugar, tamarind concentrate, ginger, pickled garlic, fish sauce, and black soy sauce. Cover the pressure cooker and cook for 45 minutes following your pressure cooker's instructions. When finished, remove from the heat, carefully release the cover to vent the steam, and open the lid. Alternatively, you can braise the dish in a large saucepan for 2 to 3 hours.

Traditionally we serve this with sticky rice; to me it's even better with Coconut and Wild Sesame Sticky Rice (page 89).

Khantoke

Literally the name of the pedestaled, lacquered tray on which the dishes are served, a *khantoke* is a traditional meal from the Lanna kingdom in northern Thailand. Offered by a host to guests at family gatherings or celebrations, the *khantoke* featured an array of small, intricate dishes, such as *gluay khaek* (see page 20), *hung lay*, and pickled vegetable relishes, to be eaten with sticky rice by hand in the Lanna style. *Khantoke* dinners remain a popular way to entertain at home, and large outdoor restaurants offering elaborate *khantoke* meals, complete with performances by dancers, drummers, and other musicians, are popular with Thais and tourists alike.

STIR-FRIED WILD BOAR WITH RED CURRY

MOO BA PAD PHET

SERVES 4

I give credit to my dad for teaching me to be adventurous. One summer he introduced me to the foragers' market, called Talad Toong Kwian, located right on a highway between Lampang and Chiang Mai. He still stops by that market all the time in search of beautiful orchids. But for me, the beauty of this market is in its abundance of hard-to-find ingredients—wild herbs, foraged mushrooms, and rare meats, including wild boar. If boar is unavailable, the aromatic herbs and rich red curry in this dish will also complement the strong flavors of lamb or venison. If you are lucky enough to find wild boar, ask your butcher to remove the tough hide for you.

2 tablespoons vegetable oil

2 tablespoons Red Curry Paste (page 229)

1 pound boneless wild boar, cut into bite-size pieces

1 cup chopped apple, Italian, or Japanese eggplant (bite-size pieces) (see Note)

1 cup long beans, cut into 1-inch pieces

3 tablespoons Thai Chicken Stock (page 236) or water

4 or 5 pieces fresh (or jarred, rinsed) peppercorns

¼ cup krachai, cut into thin julienne

1 fresh long red Thai chile, thinly sliced

2 tablespoons fish sauce, or to taste

1 tablespoon palm sugar, or to taste

4 to 5 kaffir lime leaves, torn 3 or 4 times to release their oils

¼ cup Thai basil leaves

Steamed jasmine or brown rice

Heat the oil in a wok or large sauté pan over medium-high heat. Add the curry paste and stir until fragrant, about 2 minutes, being careful not to let it burn. Add the boar, eggplant, and long beans and cook, stirring, until cooked through, 4 to 5 minutes. Stir in the stock and add the peppercorns, krachai, and chile. Gently toss for about 1 minute, until the krachai is fragrant. Stir in the fish sauce and palm sugar, remove from the heat, and add the kaffir lime leaves and Thai basil. Stir to combine well and serve over steamed jasmine or brown rice.

NOTE: If you can find pea eggplants, you might want to try them in this dish. Slightly larger than green peas, they add a juicy bitterness and great bright green color to many traditional Thai dishes.

แกงเขียวหวานไก่

ULTIMATE GREEN CURRY WITH CHICKEN

GAENG KHIAW WAN GAI

SERVES 2 TO 4

Thai people love a good party. After a long day of shooting at my parents' new farmhouse outside of Chiang Mai, one evening their neighbors surprised us all with a huge pot of delicious *gaeng khiaw wan gai* and jasmine rice, easily enough to feed the dozen of us and more. The exotic fragrance of green curry, coconut, and basil kept everyone in a great mood. Soon there was a whole party going on on the front lawn, with music, dancing, and sending up fire lanterns (this was during the lunar festival of Loi Krathong, celebrated across Thailand), culminating in fireworks and a parade to a nearby temple. It was an unforgettable night.

2 tablespoons vegetable oil or coconut cream

1 cup Green Curry Paste (page 229)

1 pound boneless chicken thighs, sliced 1 inch thick

1 (13.5-ounce) can coconut milk

1 cup cubed eggplant (½-inch cubes)

½ cup whole Thai basil leaves

¼ cup thinly sliced fresh long red Thai chiles

4 kaffir lime leaves, torn 3 or 4 times to release their oils

3 tablespoons palm sugar, or to taste

3 tablespoons fish sauce, or to taste

Steamed jasmine rice, rice noodles, or roti

In a medium saucepan, heat the oil over medium heat until sizzling (or if using coconut cream, heat it until bubbling). Add the curry paste and cook, stirring, just until fragrant and the color has intensified, about 1 minute. Watch carefully so it doesn't burn.

Add the chicken and stir to coat in the curry paste, then pour in the coconut milk and bring to a boil. Add the eggplant, lower the heat to maintain a simmer, and simmer until the chicken and eggplant are cooked through, about 8 minutes. Remove from the heat and stir in the Thai basil, chiles, and kaffir lime leaves. Stir in the sugar and fish sauce until the sugar has dissolved. Serve hot over jasmine rice or rice noodles or with roti for dipping.

BRAISED CHICKEN CHIANG MAI–STYLE

OOK GAI

SERVES 4

Ook Gai is my go-to dish when I have guests who appreciate the homey joys of a simple, rustic, and aromatic meal. The flavors bring me home and remind me of good times. It's a comforting dish, especially when served on top of fragrant jasmine rice or scooped up with a ball of freshly steamed sticky rice.

5 dried long red Thai chiles (or 8 to 10 dried Thai chiles)

Salt

1 tablespoon chopped lemongrass

2 (½-inch) slices galangal

1 teaspoon cleaned, crushed, and minced cilantro root (or 1 whole sprig cilantro, chopped)

1 teaspoon coriander seeds

⅓ cup coarsely chopped shallots

10 cloves garlic, peeled

1 tablespoon chopped fresh turmeric

2 tablespoons shrimp paste

1 tablespoon vegetable oil

1 farm-raised chicken (about 3½ pounds), cut into 8 bone-in pieces

1 quart Thai Chicken Stock (page 236)

Steamed jasmine or sticky rice

Chopped cilantro, culantro, bamboo mint, and/or scallions

Place the dried chiles in a bowl and add warm water to cover. Leave to soften for about 15 minutes. Wearing kitchen gloves (do not use bare hands when working with chiles), remove the chiles from the water and squeeze out excess water.

Using a mortar and pestle, mash the chiles with a generous pinch of salt (this keeps it from splattering). Add the lemongrass, galangal, cilantro root, and coriander seeds and continue mashing until a paste starts to form. Add the shallots, garlic, turmeric, and shrimp paste and mash into a smooth paste, about 10 minutes. Alternatively, process ingredients in a food processor for 3 to 5 minutes, until smooth and blended.

Heat the oil in a large saucepan over medium-high heat until shimmering. Add the chicken and brown it on both sides, about 4 minutes per side. Reduce the heat to medium. Stir in the paste to coat the chicken and cook, stirring, for about 2 minutes to give it some color. Add the stock, cover, and bring to a boil. Lower the heat to maintain a simmer and cook for about 20 minutes, then uncover and continue to simmer until the chicken is cooked through, about 10 minutes more.

Serve family-style over steamed jasmine or sticky rice with chopped cilantro, culantro, bamboo mint, and/or scallions.

ไส้อั่ว

CHIANG MAI SAUSAGE

SAI OOA

SERVES 4 TO 6

This is a staple of northern Thai cuisine: a minced pork seasoned with herbs, garlic, and chiles stuffed into a casing (*sai* means "intestine" and *ooa* means "to stuff"). The best way to enjoy it is with sticky rice, crispy pork skins, and *nam prik aong* (page 231). Because it's super tasty, Thais eat it both as an appetizer and entrée among other dishes at a traditional *khantoke* dinner. It would also make a great hors-d'oeuvre at a whisky party. The depth of flavor in *sai ooa* will blow you away.

5 dried Thai long red chiles, seeded

10 kaffir lime leaves, finely chopped

¼ cup sliced lemongrass

¼ cup chopped garlic

¼ cup roughly chopped shallots

2 teaspoons peeled and chopped fresh turmeric

1 tablespoon black soy sauce

2 tablespoons fish sauce

1½ teaspoons salt

2 pounds ground pork

3 sprigs cilantro, finely chopped

1 scallion, white and light green parts chopped

1 pack 1- to 1¼-inch natural sausage casing, rinsed and left to soak in a bowl of clean water (optional)

Vegetable oil if pan-searing or roasting the sausages

TO MAKE THE FILLING: Place the dried chiles in a bowl and add warm water to cover. Leave to soften for about 15 minutes. Wearing kitchen gloves (do not use bare hands when working with chiles), remove the chiles from the water and squeeze out excess water.

Using a stone mortar and pestle, pound the chiles, kaffir lime leaves, lemongrass, garlic, shallots, and turmeric into a smooth paste; this will take about 15 minutes. Alternatively, combine the ingredients in a food processor and pulse until it forms a paste, about 3 minutes. Transfer the paste to a large bowl and stir in the black soy sauce, fish sauce, and salt.

Add the pork, cilantro, and scallion to the paste and knead gently until well incorporated. Cover and refrigerate for at least 2 hours, or preferably overnight, to let the flavors marry. Heat a small amount of oil in a frying pan and brown a pinch of the filling on both sides to taste the seasoning. Adjust as needed before stuffing.

TO STUFF THE SAUSAGES (OR NOT): Affix an open end of the casing to a sausage stuffer or sausage attachment on a stand mixer. To avoid an air bubble forming at the end of the sausage, leave the end untied at first, and then tie it off with kitchen thread after the sausage is filled. Fill the casings and tie off the sausages at about 10-inch lengths. This recipe should yield about 4 sausages, depending on thickness.

If you don't have a sausage stuffer or stand mixer, fill the casings by hand: First wet your hands with a little vegetable oil or spray, then gently stuff the casing using a funnel or piping bag fitted with the widest tip. Tie off the open end after the casing begins to fill, then finish stuffing.

Your simplest option is to go without casings: Just form the sausage mixture into patties and brown them on both sides in a skillet until cooked through.

TO COOK THE SAUSAGES: There are a variety of methods of cooking the sausage; grilling over coals is the most popular and traditional.

To grill the sausages: Heat a charcoal grill to medium-low. Grill the sausages for about 10 minutes on each side, until they are lightly charred all over and the meat is no longer pink inside.

TO PAN-SEAR THE SAUSAGES: Lightly coat a large cast-iron pan with vegetable oil over medium-high heat. Add the sausages, in batches if necessary, and sear for 5 to 8 minutes on each side, until they are browned all over and the meat is no longer pink inside.

TO BOIL THE SAUSAGES: Place the sausages in a large saucepan, add cold water to cover, and bring to a boil over medium-high heat (using too much heat will cause the sausages to burst). Reduce the heat and simmer just until cooked through, about 20 minutes. Drain the boiled sausages, pat dry with paper towels, then pan-sear in a little oil in a hot pan just until browned all over.

TO ROAST THE SAUSAGES: Preheat the oven to 375°F and grease a baking sheet. Place the sausages on the baking sheet and roast, flipping once, until they are lightly browned all over and the meat is no longer pink inside, about 30 minutes.

ข้าวมันไก่

CHICKEN AND RICE

KHAO MUN GAI

SERVES 4

In Thailand you'll find this dish served at all hours—for breakfast, lunch, or as a midnight snack. It's a Chinese-inspired (or Hainanese-inspired) dish, which in Thailand usually means it has been handed down from generation to generation. I have seen the same guy making this dish at the same restaurant since I was just a little girl—it's a famous lunch spot in the heart of Chiang Mai. Last time I visited home, he was still there, serving an all-new generation of customers!

This is a simple and satisfying dish, reflected in its name: *kao* means rice, *mun* means fat, and *ghai* means chicken, or rice cooked in chicken fat.

This recipe is straightforward, created so anyone can make it at home. I especially enjoy it with Thai Miso Dipping Sauce.

FOR THE CHICKEN

- 1 whole farm-raised chicken (3 to 4 pounds)
- 4 cloves garlic, peeled
- 4 cilantro roots (or 2 bunches cilantro)
- 1 teaspoon whole black peppercorns
- 1 (2-inch) piece ginger, peeled
- Salt

FOR THE RICE

- 2 cups jasmine rice
- 2 cilantro roots, cleaned
- 2 cloves garlic, peeled
- 1 (3-inch) piece ginger, peeled and sliced

FOR THE SOUP

- 2 tablespoons light soy sauce
- 1 scallion, finely chopped
- 1 bunch cilantro, finely chopped
- Freshly ground white pepper

Thai Miso Dipping Sauce (page 235) or black soy sauce

TO COOK THE CHICKEN: In a large saucepan, bring 2 quarts of water to a boil over high heat. Carefully remove the skin and fat from chicken and set it aside. Place the chicken in the pan, add the garlic, cilantro roots, black peppercorns, and ginger, and season with salt. Return to a boil, then reduce the heat to maintain a simmer and cook for 30 minutes, until cooked through. Using tongs or a slotted spoon, remove the chicken to a large bowl, cover to keep warm, and set aside. Strain the poaching liquid for cooking the rice and discard the solids.

TO MAKE THE RICE: Coarsely chop the reserved chicken skin and fat. Heat a heavy saucepan over medium-low heat and add the skin and fat. Cover and cook for about 10 minutes, until the fat is rendered and the skin is crisp and golden.

Remove the crisped skin and discard it or snack on it as a delicious cook's treat. Pour off all but 2 to 3 tablespoons of the rendered fat from the pan and return the pan to the stovetop over medium heat.

Add the rice and stir to coat. Add the cilantro roots, garlic, and ginger and stir until well mixed. Add 2 cups of the chicken poaching liquid and bring to a boil. Reduce the heat to low to maintain a simmer, cover, and simmer for 15 minutes to cook through.

(If using a rice cooker, heat the chicken fat in a wok or a sauté pan over medium-high heat, then stir in the rice and cook for about 2 minutes to coat it in the fat. Add the cilantro roots, garlic, and ginger, and stir until well mixed. Transfer the mixture to a rice cooker and cook according to the machine's instructions.)

TO MAKE AND SERVE THE SOUP: Bring the remaining 6 cups chicken poaching liquid to a boil and add the soy sauce. Spoon into small bowls and serve garnished with the scallion, cilantro, and white pepper.

TO SERVE THE CHICKEN: Debone the chicken or slice it according to your preference and serve in individual plates over rice with Thai Miso Dipping Sauce or black soy sauce and the bowls of the soup alongside.

ปลาเผาเกลือ

GRILLED SALT-CRUSTED WHOLE FISH

PLA PHAO GLUA

SERVES 4

Before my parents decided to leave the city to start a new, slower, and healthier lifestyle on their farm, they frequented a grilled fish stall right in front of our house in downtown Chiang Mai. The seller transformed a gigantic gas tank into a charcoal grill and set up his stall right by busy Nong Hoy Street with a sign that read "salted whole grilled fish." During rush hour, many people in cars and on motorcycles would stop by and pick up the fish for family dinner. My family would just step outside to get theirs!

1 cup coarse sea salt

1 tablespoon all-purpose flour

1 (2-pound) whole bass or tilapia,
   cleaned but not scaled

1 stalk lemongrass

2 (¼-inch) pieces galangal (optional)

5 or 6 whole Thai basil leaves (optional)

Spicy Lime and Chile Sauce (page 235)

Heat a charcoal grill to medium-low.

In a medium bowl, mix the salt and flour together to fully incorporate them. Place the fish on a large cutting board or baking sheet. Insert the lemongrass stalk into the mouth of the fish and all the way to the opposite end (or as far as you can go). If you choose to use galangal and basil, stuff them into the stomach area. Rub a thin layer of the salt and flour mixture over the skin on both sides.

Place on the grill and grill for about 20 minutes on each side, until the meat turns white and opaque and is firm to the touch. Alternatively, bake the fish in a preheated 450°F oven for 25 to 30 minutes. Serve with Spicy Lime and Chile Sauce.

NOTE: To make this dish gluten free, substitute 1 egg white for the flour.

ห่อนึ่งไก่

LANNA-STYLE STEAMED CHICKEN IN BANANA LEAVES

HAW NUENG GAI

SERVES 4

Haw nueng gai is another superstar dish from northern Thailand, though it doesn't get the press other dishes such as *khao soy* and *sai ooa* do. Steaming in banana leaves is a popular method that keeps the food moist without the addition of a lot of fat, making this dish light and healthful but still full of bold, herby flavors. Don't be discouraged if you struggle at first to perfect the traditional pyramid-shaped package. The old ladies at the night market can fold them almost without looking, but no one will know if you need a few extra toothpicks to hold yours together. What you want is a good seal to keep the moisture inside the package.

5 dried long red Thai chiles (or 10 dried red Thai chiles)

5 shallots, chopped (about ¼ cup)

10 cloves garlic, chopped (about ½ cup)

1 tablespoon chopped galangal

1 stalk lemongrass (bottom 2 to 3 inches from root only), chopped

2 (2-inch) pieces fresh turmeric, chopped; or 1 tablespoon ground turmeric

Salt

2 teaspoons shrimp paste or fish sauce (optional)

2 tablespoons vegetable oil

1 pound boneless, skinless chicken breasts or thighs, thinly sliced

½ cup chopped Japanese eggplant (in ½-inch cubes)

1 small chunk of heart of palm, cut into bite-size pieces (about ½ cup; optional)

3 to 4 long beans, cut into 1-inch pieces (about ½ cup)

2 cups Thai Chicken Stock (page 236)

½ cup Toasted Rice Powder (see page 227)

7 kaffir lime leaves, torn

1 bunch cilantro, coarsely chopped

1 scallion, coarsely chopped (about 1 tablespoon)

Banana leaves, for steaming

Steamed sticky rice

Place the dried chiles in a bowl and add warm water to cover. Leave to soften for about 15 minutes. Wearing kitchen gloves (do not use bare hands when working with chiles), remove the chiles from the water and squeeze out excess water.

In a stone mortar, combine the chiles, shallots, garlic, galangal, lemongrass, and turmeric with a generous

pinch of salt and pound with a pestle until it forms a smooth paste, about 15 minutes. Alternatively, process the ingredients in a food processor until smooth, 3 to 5 minutes. Add the shrimp paste and set aside.

Heat the oil in a wok or large sauté pan over medium-high heat. Add the paste and sauté, stirring, for 3 minutes, or until very aromatic. Add chicken and

cook for 4 to 5 minutes, until halfway cooked through. Keep an eye on it—you don't want raw chicken, but you're not trying to brown it either; it will finish cooking in the steamer.

Add the eggplant, heart of palm, if using, and long beans. Cook, stirring, for 3 minutes, until vegetables soften. Add the stock, bring to a boil, then remove from the heat.

Drain off the stock and transfer the chicken mixture to a large bowl. Add the rice powder, kaffir lime leaves, cilantro, and scallion to the chicken.

Cut banana leaves into 4 sheets measuring about 6 × 10 inches to wrap and steam the filling. Place about 1 cup

of the chicken mixture into the center of each sheet and bring the long sides up and together, forming almost a cylinder. Using one hand, push the two corners of one short end out and bring the edge into the center. Fold in the remaining side and use the corners to enfold the other side, wrapping the filled leaf into a pyramid-shaped parcel. Use a toothpick to hold the package closed and keep the filling moist as it steams.

Set up a double boiler with a steamer insert, adding water to come about 2 inches up the side of the steamer, and bring to a boil over high heat. Place the banana leaf parcels in the steamer and cover and steam until the banana leaves start to turn a golden yellow-brown at the edges, about 10 minutes. Serve with sticky rice.

ไก่ทอดเที่ยงคืน

MIDNIGHT FRIED CHICKEN

GAI TOD TIANG KUEN

SERVES 2 TO 4

The love for fried chicken is universal. This recipe is inspired by a famous fried chicken shack that opens at midnight and is a staple of Chiang Mai nightlife. It's the perfect place for long evenings when folks get hungry again well after dinner.

The best way to enjoy my take on this dish is with your hands—no utensils! Grab some sticky rice, crispy pork rinds, Northern–Style Pork and Cherry Tomato Relish (page 231), and a few cold beers, turn on your favorite music, invite your favorite people, and it's an instant party. And luckily no one has to turn into a pumpkin after hours! You can easily multiply this recipe to serve a hungry crowd.

1 whole farm-raised chicken (3 pounds),
    cut into 8 pieces

2 cups Ngam's House Marinade (page 227)

4 quarts vegetable oil

2 cups all-purpose flour

Salt

In a large bowl, toss the chicken with Ngam's House Marinade to coat and let sit for at least 45 minutes or even overnight in the refrigerator.

Heat the oil in a large high-sided skillet over medium heat to 375°F.

As the oil is coming up to temperature, dredge the chicken pieces in the flour to evenly coat them. Using tongs or a slotted spoon, carefully add the pieces to the hot oil and fry until crisp, 8 to 10 minutes on each side, or about 20 minutes total. Transfer the chicken to a wire rack to drain, immediately season with salt, and serve.

MOM'S BEST BABY BACK RIBS

SEE KLONG MOO TOD

SERVES 4

Even now as a professional cook, homemade meals are my favorite, especially when they're from my family's kitchen. This ribs recipe is dear to my heart. If it had been up to me, I'd have had them for dinner every single night growing up!

6 cilantro roots, cleaned and chopped

3 cloves garlic, smashed and chopped

1 teaspoon whole white peppercorns

¼ cup fish sauce

2 tablespoons turbinado sugar

2 pounds baby back ribs, cleaned and cut into 2-inch pieces (ask your butcher to do this)

2 quarts vegetable oil

Hot steamed jasmine, brown, or sticky rice

10 to 12 fried kaffir lime leaves (optional; see Note)

In a stone mortar, combine the cilantro roots, garlic, and white peppercorns and pound with a pestle until it forms a paste, about 3 minutes. Transfer to a large bowl and stir in the fish sauce and sugar. Add the ribs, cover, and marinate in the refrigerator for about 45 minutes or up to overnight.

In a wok or a medium saucepan, heat the oil over medium-high heat until it reaches 375°F. Add the ribs and fry until golden brown, about 5 minutes. Using tongs, remove the ribs to a baking sheet lined with paper towels to drain.

Serve with rice. Top with fried kaffir lime leaves, if using.

NOTE: Have you ever fried sage or basil leaves for an added aromatic crunch? Much the same way, Thai cooks love to crisp up kaffir lime leaves in hot oil to add another flavorful component to dishes like this one. Simply bring a small deep saucepan of oil to 350°F over medium-high heat, add dry kaffir lime leaves and fry gently for 1 to 2 minutes, just until the leaves crisp and turn a glossy, dark color.

ไข่พะโล้

MY CHILDHOOD FAVORITE: EGGS AND PORK BELLY

KHAI PALOW

SERVES 4

As a kid, I was an easygoing eater. I would eat anything as long as it contained eggs—boiled, scrambled, sunny side up, you name it. Over time I got a bit more sophisticated and quickly fell for this comforting dish of eggs paired with pork belly stewed in a cinnamon and five-spice powder–scented broth. I could never say no to it!

3 medium cilantro roots, cleaned and
    finely chopped

5 large cloves garlic, finely chopped

2 teaspoons whole white peppercorns

2 pounds pork belly, cut into 2-inch cubes

5 pieces star anise

5 cinnamon sticks

2 teaspoons five-spice powder

8 eggs

2 quarts vegetable oil

10 ounces firm tofu, cut into 1-inch cubes

½ cup palm sugar

2 quarts water

½ cup fish sauce

2 tablespoons sweet black soy sauce

1 tablespoon light soy sauce

Hot steamed jasmine or brown rice

In a stone mortar, combine the cilantro roots, garlic, and white peppercorns and pound with a pestle into a coarse paste. Transfer to a large bowl. Add the pork belly, star anise, cinnamon sticks, and five-spice powder and mix well to coat, then chill in the refrigerator for 30 minutes.

While the pork is marinating, place the eggs in a saucepan large enough to hold them in single layer and add cold water to cover by 1 inch. Turn the heat to high and bring just to a boil. Remove from the heat, cover the pan, and leave for 12 minutes. Transfer the eggs to a cold-water bath to stop the cooking. Once the eggs are cool enough to handle, remove them from the water and peel, dry, and set them aside.

Heat the oil in a large high-sided skillet over high heat until it reaches 375°F. Add the tofu and fry until golden brown, 3 to 5 minutes. Remove with a slotted spoon to a plate lined with paper towels and set aside.

Place the sugar in a medium saucepan over medium heat and heat until it starts to caramelize and forms large bubbles, about 5 minutes, being careful not to let it burn. Add the pork and cook, stirring, for about 5 minutes, until the pork is halfway cooked through. Add the water, fish sauce, sweet black soy sauce, light soy sauce, hard-boiled eggs, and tofu. Bring to a simmer and simmer for 1 hour, till the eggs are brown and the pork belly is tender. Serve hot with jasmine or brown rice.

แอ๊บปลา

NORTHERN THAI–STYLE GRILLED FISH IN BANANA LEAVES

AB PLA

SERVES 2

My dad's extended family lives in the Lampoon province, in a small town about an hour south of Chiang Mai. Growing up, we drove there to visit my aunt most every weekend, and we'd almost always stop by the town's famous northern Thai restaurant for this dish. I was like a moth that was more than happy to fly into that delicious flame. While I don't get to Lampoon very often these days, making this dish at home is almost like being there again.

5 dried long red Thai chiles

1 small shallot, roughly chopped

2 medium cloves garlic, chopped

¼ cup chopped lemongrass (from 2 stalks, bottom 2 to 3 inches from the root)

5 kaffir lime leaves

1 teaspoon coriander seeds, toasted

1 small knob fresh turmeric, chopped; or ¼ teaspoon dried turmeric

1 teaspoon salt, plus more for seasoning the fish

1 pound fish fillets, such as catfish, snakehead, or red snapper

½ cup whole Thai basil leaves

1 to 2 fresh Thai chiles, cut in half lengthwise

2 fresh banana leaves

Hot steamed sticky rice

Place the dried chiles in a bowl and add warm water to cover. Leave to soften for about 15 minutes. Wearing kitchen gloves (do not use bare hands when working with chiles), remove the chiles from the water and squeeze out excess water.

In a stone mortar, combine the chiles, shallot, garlic, lemongrass, 2 of the kaffir lime leaves, the coriander, turmeric, and salt and pound with a pestle into a smooth paste, about 15 minutes. Alternatively, process the ingredients in food processor for 5 minutes, until smooth. Set aside.

Heat a charcoal grill to medium heat.

In a medium bowl, rub the fish fillets all over with the paste and season with salt. Set aside on the counter to marinate for 30 minutes.

Cut the banana leaves into two 10-inch squares. Place half of the fish in the center of each leaf and top with the Thai basil, the remaining kaffir lime leaf cut into chiffonade, and the chiles. Fold the leaves around the fish to make a parcel and carefully secure the edges with a toothpick so the banana leaves can hold in the moisture as the fish grills.

Once the coals are ready, reduce the heat to medium-low and grill over direct heat until the fish is cooked through, turning once, about 20 minutes. Transfer to a platter, carefully unfold the charred banana leaf wrapper, and serve with sticky rice.

NOTE: In Thailand we use small freshwater fish for this recipe, or sometimes you may see Ab with pork or even pork brain. I guess we are adventurous when it comes to food!

ลาบหมูเชียงใหม่

PORK *LAAB*

LAAB MOO CHIANG MAI

SERVES 2 TO 4

I am such a daddy's girl. I walk like him, talk like him, and my friends in high school used to tease me that I even would drive like him. One of my favorite memories is hopping on the back of his motorcycle and going to the local market together. The market equals yummy food, and yummy food equals happiness! My dad seemed to know all the market vendors, but his favorite was an older lady who sold a mean *laab*. Dad would buy all the raw ingredients and cook it at home for my brother and me. I'll never forget how he taught us how to eat *laab*: roll your sticky rice into a small ball, dip it in the *laab*, and pop it in your mouth. Dad knows best!

1 pound ground pork

5 ounces pork liver, thinly sliced (optional; if not using add additional ground pork)

1 tablespoon *Laab* Chile (recipe follows), or to taste

½ cup vegetable oil

¼ cup chopped garlic

2 to 3 dried Thai red chiles

2 tablespoons chopped lemongrass

5 kaffir lime leaves, cut into thin chiffonade

Leaves from 2 sprigs mint, cut into thin chiffonade

Leaves from 2 sprigs bamboo mint, cut into thin chiffonade

Leaves from 3 sprigs culantro, cut into thin chiffonade

4 scallions, thinly sliced

1 sprig cilantro, finely chopped

2 tablespoons fish sauce, or to taste

For garnish: thinly sliced kaffir lime leaves, thinly sliced lemongrass and shallots, crispy pork rinds, chopped cilantro, chopped scallions, cucumber slices, cherry tomatoes, long beans, cabbage leaves

In a large bowl, combine the ground pork and liver with the *laab* chile until just mixed. Set aside.

In a wide sauté pan, heat ¼ cup of the oil over low heat. Add the garlic and cook slowly until golden and fragrant, watching carefully so it doesn't burn, about 3 minutes. Transfer the crispy garlic and oil to a small bowl and set aside.

Add the remaining ¼ cup oil to the pan, add the chiles, and cook until darkened in color, about 2 minutes. Transfer the crispy chiles and oil to a second small bowl and set aside.

In the same pan over medium-high heat, sauté the pork mixture just until no longer pink, about 3 minutes. Add 1 tablespoon of the fried garlic along with the lemongrass and kaffir lime leaves and cook until fragrant, about 1 minute. Stir in the two kinds of mint, the culantro, scallions, and cilantro and cook, stirring, for another 2 minutes, until fragrant. Off the heat, season with fish sauce to taste.

Transfer to a platter and garnish with kaffir lime leaves, lemongrass, shallots, crispy pork rinds, the remaining fried garlic, the fried chiles, chopped cilantro, and scallions. Serve with cucumber and cherry tomatoes.

LAAB CHILE

MAKES ½ CUP

4 dried red Thai chiles, or to taste

1 teaspoon whole black peppercorns

1 teaspoon coriander seeds

2 pieces star anise

1 teaspoon Szechuan peppercorns

1 teaspoon whole cloves

2 cinnamon sticks, broken into pieces

5 pieces dried *dee plee* peppers (see page 242)

1 whole nutmeg

1 teaspoon cardamom pods

1 teaspoon salt

Toast all the ingredients except for the salt in a medium sauté pan over medium-low heat until aromatic, 2 to 3 minutes. Transfer to a mortar and pestle and let cool completely. Add the salt and pound with a pestle into a fine powder. (If you don't have a mortar and pestle, you can use a spice grinder.) The *laab* chile will keep in an airtight container for up to 1 month.

RED FIRE WATER SPINACH

PAD PAK BOONG FAI DAENG

SERVES 2 TO 4

I have wonderful memories in the kitchen with my mother. I still remember her telling me that when it comes to stir-frying, you have to prepare your ingredients first and have everything ready so that once the oil is hot, you can cook everything right away so your vegetables will keep their crunch and not get wilted.

You might be wondering why I call this dish Red Fire Water Spinach. Well, if you were to see the big flames coming from the wok in the night market, you'd know right away. Here I show you how to make it the way they do at the market, but don't burn your house down just for spinach! If you don't want the big flame, make it without the extra ladleful of oil I add in the alternate version and the vegetables will still cook perfectly.

2 tablespoons vegetable oil

1 pound water spinach, washed and trimmed

1 clove garlic, smashed and finely chopped

2 to 3 fresh long red Thai chiles, thinly sliced,
   or 1 regular Thai chile, smashed

2 tablespoons Thai miso

1 teaspoon sugar

¼ cup water or Thai Chicken Stock (page 236)

In a large sauté pan or wok, heat the oil over very high heat.

In a medium bowl, combine the water spinach, garlic, chiles, Thai miso, and sugar. Once the oil hits the smoking point, throw everything into the pan and sauté, stirring, for about 1 minute, until the water spinach is just softened. Transfer to plates and serve.

NOTE: While perhaps not for the novice chef, to make the most authentic red fire spinach, try a go at this (you'll want to observe all sensible precautions for cooking with fire, making sure you have proper ventilation and a fire extinguisher at the ready):

In a sauté pan or wok, heat the 2 tablespoons oil over very high heat.

Fill a small ladle with a little more oil and hold it in one hand. In a medium bowl, combine the water spinach, garlic, chiles, Thai miso, and sugar and hold the bowl with the other hand. Once the oil in the pan reaches the smoking point, very carefully add the water spinach mixture and the ladleful of oil into the pan at the same time. There will be a big fire. Step back. Once the initial flame dies down (this will happen right away), sauté, stirring, until the water spinach is just wilted, about 1 minute. Transfer to plates and serve.

ถั่วลันเตาผัดน้ำมันหอย

SAUTÉED SUGAR SNAP PEAS WITH OYSTER SAUCE

TUA LAN TAO PAD NAM MUN HOY

SERVES 4

This is one of my family's favorite recipes. My mom would ask me to help her clean the peas, and as I did so, she would act as if she were the star of her own cooking show. We could have called it *Five-Minute Dishes* because in less than five minutes, we'd have a side dish that was sweet, crisp, and super tasty.

2 tablespoons vegetable oil

2 large cloves garlic, smashed and coarsely chopped

2 cups sugar snap peas, trimmed

2 tablespoons oyster sauce

1 teaspoon sugar

½ to 1 teaspoon ground white pepper, to taste

In a wok or medium sauté pan, heat the oil until just smoking. Add the garlic, snap peas, oyster sauce, and sugar and sauté, stirring, until the green of the peas intensifies but they remain crunchy, 1 to 2 minutes. Transfer the peas to a plate, sprinkle with the white pepper, and serve.

ข้าวหนุกงา

COCONUT AND WILD SESAME STICKY RICE

KHAO NOOK NGA

SERVES 2

Mom introduced me to this rice recipe, and from the first bite, I've never looked back. Its sweet coconut-y crunch and just a hint of salt make this a great complement to northern Thai braised dishes such as Braised Pork Belly in *Hung Lay* Curry (page 54), Braised Chicken Chiang Mai–Style (page 63)—just about anything from Chiang Mai!

1 tablespoon wild sesame seeds, toasted (see Note)

½ teaspoon salt

1 cup cooked sticky rice

2 tablespoons coconut milk

In a stone mortar or sturdy mixing bowl, use the pestle to coarsely crush the wild sesame seeds. Sprinkle with the salt and crush until combined. Add the sticky rice and coconut milk and knead with the pestle until well mixed, about 2 minutes.

NOTE: Wild sesame seeds are actually perilla seeds, which come from a relative of *shiso* in the mint family also common in Japanese and Korean cuisine. Darker brown and fatter than sesame seeds, they have a similar aromatic, nutty flavor with herbal notes. Wild sesame seeds can be found online, in Asian or Korean groceries, or specialty spice markets. Black sesame seeds make a fine substitute.

ข้าวเหนียวมะม่วง

COCONUT STICKY RICE WITH MANGO

KHAO NIAW MAMUANG

SERVES 2 TO 4

First things first: You don't *make* sticky rice sticky, you buy *kao niaw*, or glutinous rice, and cook it. Sticky rice is a common ingredient in Asian markets, so making your own starts with a simple trip down to your local Chinatown. There are two kinds of sticky rice: white and black. I find the black variety to have a slightly deeper, nuttier flavor, though either works for this recipe. *Khao niaw mamuang* is easily the most popular Thai dessert and the most requested one when I entertain at home and at Ngam. Sweet and juicy ripe mango is key to balance the nutty flavor and chewy bite of the sticky rice, and the trick to perfect sticky rice—fragrant, flavorful, not mushy—is to steam it until just al dente then let the rice soak up the fragrant liquid. Remember you'll need to soak your sticky rice for at least six hours before cooking.

1½ cups uncooked glutinous rice

1 (13.5-ounce) can coconut milk

½ cup palm sugar

1 teaspoon jasmine extract

Pinch of salt

1 to 2 sweet ripe mangos

Soak the rice in a bowl with room-temperature water to cover for at least 6 hours or overnight. Drain and discard the soaking liquid.

Prepare a rice steamer or a double boiler with a steamer insert lined with cheesecloth, adding water to come about 2 inches up the sides of the steamer. Bring the water in the steamer to a boil over high heat, add the rice and wrap with the cheesecloth, cover, then lower the heat to medium-high and steam the until the rice is just al dente, about 15 minutes. Transfer to a large bowl.

While the rice is steaming, in a small saucepan, combine the coconut milk, sugar, jasmine extract, and salt and heat over low heat, stirring, until the sugar is dissolved.

Pour the warm coconut milk mixture over the rice and gently fold the liquid into the rice until well mixed. Place plastic wrap directly on top of the rice and let sit, covered, until the rice absorbs most of the coconut milk, about 30 minutes. Transfer the remaining coconut milk mixture to a small bowl for serving.

When you're ready to serve, peel, pit, and slice the mango, as desired. Unwrap the sticky rice and divide it among serving plates. Serve with the sliced mango and drizzle the rice with the remaining coconut milk mixture or pass it at the table.

NOTE: Using half white sticky rice and half black sticky rice gives the finished dish a rich purple hue. Add an extra 10 minutes to your cooking time.

JASMINE COCONUT JELLY

WOON GRATI

MAKES ABOUT 16 (2-INCH) CUBES

I grew up in a compound house, which meant that I never ran out of friends to play with! The compound was so big that we had many food vendors who would come right to our home on a regular basis. There was the guy who drove a motorcycle with a fruit cart on the back in the afternoon and the *roti* guy who would come at night, but the most memorable of the vendors was the guy with the dessert bicycle-truck who came when we had larger parties. He always had lots and lots of Thai sweets displayed in square trays. The most popular were *sankhaya* (Thai custard), *tong yip*, *tong yod*, *foi tong* (all to-die-for old-school egg-based Thai candies), different varieties of sweet sticky rice, and my favorite, *woon grati*. I was always so indecisive, especially with so many mouthwatering choices in front of me, but these sweet, refreshing, and super-fragrant jasmine coconut jellies were more often than not my choice. The dessert bicycle is less common in Thailand these days, but that won't stop you from making your own *woot grati* at home.

2 tablespoons agar-agar powder

4 cups coconut milk

1 cup sugar

1 teaspoon jasmine extract

1 cup young coconut meat sliced into small strips
   (optional)

In a medium saucepan, whisk the agar-agar into the coconut milk until dissolved. Place over low heat and bring to a boil, stirring often. Add the sugar and jasmine extract and continue to stir until the sugar is dissolved. Remove from the heat and add the young coconut meat, if using.

Strain the jelly mixture into an 8 × 9-inch tray, shaped pan of your choice, or individual cups. Cool in the refrigerator until set, about 3 hours. Before serving, run a thin-bladed knife around the edge of shaped molds or simply slice squares from the tray.

NOTE: In the old days, cooks would use cleaned unbloomed jasmine to infuse rainwater overnight; when the jasmine would bloom, it would release its fragrance into the water.

ผลไม้รวมและพริกกับเกลือ

SEASONAL FRUIT
WITH CANDIED SALTED CHILES

PON LA MAI RUAM LEH PRIK GUB GLUA

MAKES ABOUT ¼ CUP

A pretty wonderful fact of life of growing up in Thailand is the abundance of fruit. With a huge variety growing all over the country from the north to the south to the northeast and central Thailand, it is no surprise that fruit vendors and fruit carts are found everywhere. One thing we Thais love to do with fruit is to serve with it with *prik gub glua*, or chiles and salt. I like to add a sweet element to this mix, and I call my version candied salted chile. It's my favorite garnish for any fruit plate.

3 fresh red Thai chiles

¼ cup brown sugar

1½ tablespoons sea salt

2 pounds ripe fruit, such as cored and sliced pineapple, apples, green mango, whole strawberries, dragonfruit, and sliced guava, depending on preference and season

Place the chiles in a stone mortar and pound with a pestle into pieces—you want to break the chiles apart so they mix with the sugar and salt, not pulverize them into pulp, but some mashing is fine. Add the brown sugar and salt and use the pestle to gently coat the chiles with the sugar and salt. Place in a bowl, dip slices of fruit of choice into the candied salted chiles and enjoy out of hand.

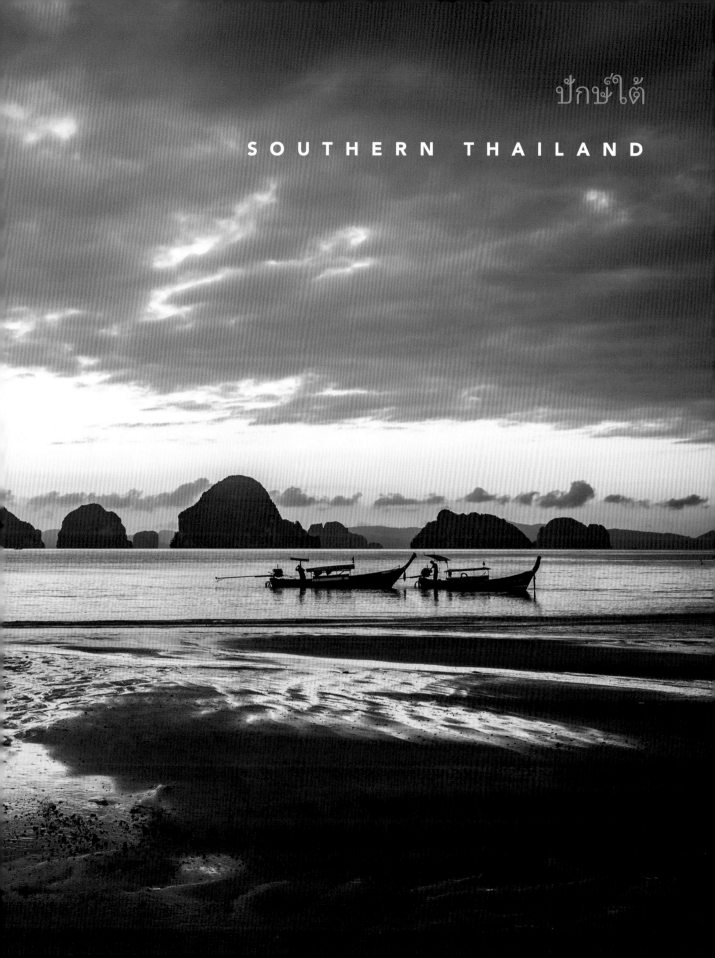

ปักษ์ใต้

SOUTHERN THAILAND

ปักษ์ใต้

SOUTHERN THAILAND

Salted Eggs
Khai Khem

Tom Yum with Shrimp
and Young Coconut
Tom Yum Koong Maprow On

Mango and Crab Salad
Yum Mamuang

Grilled Hanger Steak Salad
Yum Nua Yang

Southern-Style Mussel Curry
Gaeng Hoi Malaeng Pooh Kup
Sapparot

Dancing Calamari
Pla Meuk Pad Cha

Grilled Mixed Seafood with
Spicy Lime and Chile Sauce
Talay Pao Kup Nam Jim Seafood

Sautéed Crab with Egg
and Curry Sauce
Boo Pad Pong Garee

Southern-Style Deep-Fried
Whole Fish
Pla Tod Khamin

Stinky Beans with Shrimp
Sataw Pad Goong

Grandma's Rice Bowl
Khao Yum

ไข่เค็ม

SALTED EGGS

KHAI KHEM

MAKES 12 EGGS

This dish always reminds me of sixth grade home economics class, when we learned how to preserve food by making salted eggs. It was so much fun, and I was so impatient to taste my homemade salted eggs. It felt like the longest two weeks of my life! When the wait was over, I brought the jar of eggs home and proudly presented it to my family, and we ate them with rice porridge. My favorite part is the yolk, because it tastes nutty, but the salty white is delicious too.

12 fresh duck or chicken eggs

2 cups salt

2 quarts water

Gently but thoroughly rinse the eggs and set aside.

In a large saucepan, bring the water to a boil and add the salt. Once the salt has dissolved, remove from the heat and let the water cool to room temperature.

Gently put the eggs in a large clean container or two smaller containers that can seal, such as mason jars, and pour the cooled brine over them. The eggs must be submerged in the brine and kept in a dark place, such as a cupboard or cabinet, at room temperature for 14 to 20 days, depending on how briny and creamy you prefer your salted eggs (longer for more).

When you're ready to cook your eggs, fill a saucepan nearly full with cold water. Add the desired number of eggs, bring the water to a gentle boil over medium-high heat, and boil for 10 minutes. Remove each egg from the water using a slotted spoon and let cool. Use a knife to cut the egg in half lengthwise through the shell, scoop the egg out, and serve.

NOTE: These eggs are salty, savory, and delicious on their own, but I love to turn them into a spicy salad by squeezing some lime juice over a couple of chopped salted eggs and topping them with sliced Thai chiles, shallots, and roughly chopped cilantro.

ต้มยำกุ้งมะพร้าวอ่อน

TOM YUM WITH SHRIMP AND YOUNG COCONUT

TOM YUM KOONG MAPROW ON

SERVES 4 TO 6

My mom grew up in the south, which is why our family traveled there often. One of my favorite memories comes from one such trip, a day I remember sitting on a deserted beach after fun in the ocean with my family. That night we were drinking fresh coconut water and had had the freshest seafood you could imagine. This soup captures it all and takes me right back there. The young coconut juice and meat give the soup a deep coconut flavor that balances the spiciness of the Thai chiles.

1 quart coconut water

1 cilantro root, cleaned

3 stalks lemongrass, cut into ¼-inch slices

1 (2-inch) piece galangal

¼ cup cherry tomatoes, cut in half

3 ounces oyster mushrooms (about 1 cup), sliced

8 ounces large shrimp

3 fresh red Thai chiles, or to taste, bruised

½ cup lime juice

½ cup fish sauce

10 Kaffir lime leaves, torn in half

1 sprig cilantro, coarsely chopped

1 scallion, white and light green parts coarsely chopped

4 (1-inch) strips young coconut meat, scooped from 1 fresh coconut or canned coconut

In a medium saucepan, bring the coconut water just to a boil over medium heat, then reduce the heat to a maintain a gentle simmer. Add the cilantro root, lemongrass, galangal, tomatoes, and mushrooms, followed by the shrimp and chiles.

Raise the heat to high to bring to a boil again; boil just until the shrimp are cooked through, about 2 minutes. Remove from the heat, add the lime juice and fish sauce, and stir. Add the kaffir lime leaves, cilantro, scallion, and coconut meat and stir again. Spoon into bowls and serve.

ยำมะม่วง

MANGO AND CRAB SALAD

YUM MAMUANG

SERVES 4

This may be my favorite summertime salad. Its balance of sweet, sour, salty, and spicy flavors among only a few choice ingredients is quintessentially Thai. Try it with either ripe or green mango, depending on your preference.

1 ripe or green mango, peeled, pitted, and cut into julienne (about 2 cups)

1 cup lump crabmeat, preferably blue crab

2 tablespoons thinly sliced shallot

2 tablespoons finely chopped fresh cilantro

½ cup Spicy Lime and Chile Sauce (page 235)

2 tablespoons chopped young coconut meat (optional)

2 tablespoons toasted unsweetened coconut flakes

2 tablespoons toasted and coarsely chopped cashews or peanuts

In a large bowl, lightly toss the mango, crab, shallot, cilantro, Spicy Lime and Chile Sauce, and young coconut meat, if using. Transfer to a serving platter, top with the toasted coconut flakes and cashews, and serve.

ยำเนื้อย่าง

GRILLED HANGER STEAK SALAD

YUM NUA YANG

SERVES 4 TO 6

I love the refreshingly sweet note of local seasonal fruits paired with the savory flavor of a good piece of steak. Most of all, I love the spicy and aromatic Thai flavor combination of chiles, lime, mint, and cilantro. This dish is a combination of my favorite ingredients, and eating it is like listening to a symphony of sweet and spicy notes. Best of all, you can change the tune of the song with the seasons. How delicious!

1 pound hanger steak

½ cup Ngam's House Marinade (page 227)

1 cup ripe fruit (cut into bite-size pieces), such as grapes, plums, apples, or honeydew melon (see Note)

½ cup cherry tomato halves

1 small shallot, thinly sliced

¼ cup mint leaves

¼ cup cilantro (optional)

½ cup Simple Thai Salad Dressing (page 237)

In a large bowl, toss the steak with the marinade and set aside on the counter for 30 minutes or up to 2 hours in the refrigerator.

Heat a charcoal grill to medium-high heat. Grill the steak on one side over direct heat for 4 minutes, then turn and continue grilling over indirect heat for another 3 to 5 minutes for medium-rare or up to 10 more minutes for medium-well, as desired. Rest the meat on a cutting board for 5 to 10 minutes to let the juices settle, then thinly slice it against the grain.

In a large bowl, mix the sliced steak with the remaining ingredients, divide among bowls, and serve.

NOTE: Using fruit in season ensures the best quality and flavor. In the summer months, my favorites for this recipe include fresh berries, grapes, mango (both green and yellow), and honeydew, cantaloupe, and even watermelon. In the fall, apples and pears add delicious crunch.

แกงหอยแมลงภู่กับสับปะรด

SOUTHERN-STYLE MUSSEL CURRY

GAENG HOI MALAENG POOH KUP SAPPAROT

SERVES 4

Even though I grew up in the north of Thailand, I have a deep love for the fiery southern Thai flavors from my mother's side. This dish is close to my heart—sweet from the coconut milk, pineapple, and mussels, aromatic from the kaffir lime leaves and other herbs, and spicy from the curry paste. The palm sugar and fish sauce round it out at the end, bringing a balance to the whole dish that is very Thai. For ease and a little extra elegance, remove the mussels from their shells before serving.

1 cup Red Curry Paste (page 229)

1 (13.5-ounce) can coconut milk

1 pound mussels, cleaned

2 cups diced fresh pineapple

6 to 8 kaffir lime leaves, torn

2 tablespoons palm sugar, or to taste
    (depending on the sweetness of the pineapple)

2 tablespoons fish sauce

Hot steamed jasmine or brown rice

In a wok or medium pot, combine the curry paste with 2 tablespoons of the coconut cream. Heat over medium heat, stirring until fully incorporated and the mixture is fragrant, about 2 minutes. Add the mussels and stir to coat with the curry paste for 1 minute.

Add the remaining coconut milk, the pineapple, and kaffir lime leaves and cook, stirring occasionally, until well mixed and heated through, about 3 minutes.

Add the sugar and fish sauce and bring to a boil. Reduce the heat to maintain a simmer and cook until the flavors have combined and all the mussels have opened (discard any that haven't), about 5 minutes. Serve over steamed jasmine or brown rice.

ปลาหมึกผัดฉ่า

DANCING CALAMARI

PLA MEUK PAD CHA

SERVES 4

As much of a pleasure and an honor as it was to lead my team across Thailand, cooking, eating, shopping, and photographing various dishes, locations, and sights, it was a lot of responsibility, a lot of traveling, and a lot of work! Toward the end of the trip, after almost two weeks, I knew we needed a fun break. I'd secured us a villa in Phuket, right on the beach. It was so beautiful and tranquil, but we needed to dance! We cranked up some fantastic dance music my makeup and hair stylist had with him and cut loose. We danced off all the frustration, tension, and weariness and laughed together like kids. Later that evening I whipped up this dish, and the exciting, spicy, tangy flavors from the chiles, krachai, peppercorns, and basil got the party started all over again. Sometimes you just need to dance!

2 cloves garlic, smashed

1 to 2 fresh red Thai chiles, smashed

Salt if needed

1 tablespoon vegetable oil

10 ounces calamari, cleaned, large pieces scored in crosshatch

1 fresh long red Thai chile, sliced into ¼-inch rounds

¼ cup thinly sliced krachai

2 strands fresh peppercorns

½ cup chopped Thai basil leaves

1 tablespoon oyster sauce

2 teaspoons fish sauce

Combine the garlic and smashed chile in a mortar and pound with a pestle until coarsely crushed. Alternatively, finely chop the garlic and chile together with a chef's knife, adding a little salt and pressing with the flat side of the knife to crush.

In a wok or medium skillet, heat the oil over medium heat. Add the crushed garlic and chile and stir until fragrant, 1 to 2 minutes, watching carefully so they don't burn. Add the calamari and cook, stirring, until half cooked through and partly opaque, about 3 minutes. Add the sliced chile, the krachai, peppercorns, and Thai basil, then the oyster sauce and fish sauce and stir to coat. Cook until the calamari is fully cooked but not browned, about 3 minutes.

ทะเลเผากับน้ำจิ้มซีฟู้ด

GRILLED MIXED SEAFOOD WITH SPICY LIME AND CHILE SAUCE

TALAY PAO KUP NAM JIM SEAFOOD

Grilling seafood can seem tricky, but needn't be. To cook the fish through and impart that great smoky flavor, I prefer direct medium heat over a charcoal grill.

Variety of grilled mixed seafood (see below)
Spicy Lime and Chile Sauce (page 235)

WHOLE FISH: Don't let the idea of grilling whole fish intimidate you. First, get the freshest fish you can from your local, trustworthy market or fishmonger (or best yet, straight off the boat). Make sure the eyes are clear, gills still pink or red, and that they smell of the sea, not of fish. My favorite fish to grill are whole sea bass, red snapper, and branzino. Ask to have the fish cleaned and scaled so they're ready to use when you get home.

For the grill, you can use banana leaves (see page 80) or aluminum foil to wrap the fish—this prevents the skin from burning or sticking to the grill. If you like, you can stuff the fish with herbs such as lemongrass stalks, slices of galangal, or Thai basil leaves. Most whole fish will cook through after about 10 minutes on each side (don't be concerned if banana leaves char on the outside before the fish is done; that will give the fish great smoky flavor).

SHRIMP, PRAWNS, AND LOBSTER: There are many ways to cook these. If the shrimp or prawns are extra large and the shells are hard, I love grilling directly over the fire with the shells kept on. These usually will take about 6 minutes to cook (3 minutes on each side). For smaller shrimp out of the shell, use two skewers to hold them together; use metal skewers, or soak wooden skewers in water for a few hours so they don't burn. Smaller shrimp should take about

4 minutes to cook (2 minutes on each side). For lobsters I suggest you cut them in half and grill them, shell side down, directly over the heat for 8 to 10 minutes.

CLAMS, COCKLES, OYSTERS, AND MUSSELS: These little guys are great for grilling. The rule of thumb is you will know when they are cooked when the shells pop open, after about 10 minutes. Before grilling, make sure you clean them well! Big ones can go directly onto the grill, but for small clams or cockles I make an open packet out of aluminum foil so they don't slip through the grate.

CALAMARI: Calamari has a tendency to turn rubbery or tough on the grill, so I use a paring knife to score the bodies to help it stay tender. Grill until the flesh is just opaque and lightly charred in spots, 2 to 3 minutes. Keep it simple with salt or use Ngam's House Marinade (page 227) to season before grilling.

CRABS: There's no magic trick to grilling crabs, except to choose the freshest ones possible, clean them well, and grill over direct medium heat for about 10 minutes. One thing to keep in mind, both for cooking and for handling, is that the shells will get hot and hold on to that heat, so the crabs will finish cooking after they are removed from the grill—so keep your eyes on the shells. Like lobster, crab shells grow pink or red when they are done, a handy natural indicator.

SAUTÉED CRAB
WITH EGG AND CURRY SAUCE

BOO PAD PONG GAREE

SERVES 4

This savory custardlike sauce is a perfect pairing for fresh crab—Maryland blue, stone, or even king crab. Jumbo Maryland blue crabs are like the *poo ma* crabs that I grew up eating in Thailand. The sweetness of coconut milk and eggs with fragrant curry powder will surely entice you to make it again and again next time crabs are in season.

2 large eggs

½ cup coconut milk

1 tablespoon Madras curry powder

1 tablespoon chile jam (*nam prik pao*)

1 tablespoon vegetable oil

2 cloves garlic, smashed and chopped

2 fresh jumbo Maryland blue crabs, cleaned, trimmed, quartered, and cracked

2 teaspoons mushroom sauce

1 tablespoon oyster sauce

1 teaspoon sugar

3 stalks Chinese celery, chopped

2 scallions, cut into 1-inch pieces

1 fresh long red Thai chile

Hot steamed jasmine or brown rice

In a small bowl, whisk the eggs, coconut milk, curry powder, and chile jam to combine. Set aside.

Heat the oil in a wok or large skillet over medium heat. Add the garlic and sauté, stirring, until fragrant and golden, about 2 minutes. Add the crab and cook, stirring, until the shells turn bright orange and the meat turns white, about 4 minutes. Pour in the egg mixture, the mushroom sauce, oyster sauce, and sugar and mix to coat. Stir in the Chinese celery, scallions, and chile and toss just until the vegetables wilt, about 2 minutes. Serve over jasmine or brown rice.

ปลาทอดขมิ้น

SOUTHERN-STYLE DEEP-FRIED WHOLE FISH

PLA TOD KHAMIN

SERVES 4

This recipe makes magic happen: I have seen an entire fish disappear right in front of my eyes! As involved as deep-frying a whole fish may sound, the ingredients are all quite accessible and the technique is simple. Forget about setting the table, though—just tell everyone to use clean hands. It'll vanish like magic.

3 (2-inch) pieces fresh turmeric

4 to 5 cloves garlic, peeled

4 to 5 cilantro roots, cleaned
  (or 4 to 5 sprigs cilantro)

1 teaspoon whole white peppercorns

2 teaspoons salt

2 quarts vegetable oil

1 (1½- to 2-pound) whole sea bass (see Note),
  deboned, cleaned, and patted dry

Spicy Lime and Chile Sauce (page 235)

Combine the turmeric, garlic, cilantro roots, white peppercorns, and salt in a stone mortar and pound with a pestle into a paste.

Rub the fish all over with the turmeric paste.

In a large wok or a wide pot, heat the oil over medium-high heat to 375°F (or until it makes a crackling noise when you drop a small piece of rub into the oil).

Carefully lay the fish in the wok and fry until the skin is golden brown, about 5 minutes. If your vessel is large enough to submerge the whole fish in the oil, you don't need to flip or turn the fish as it cooks; if not, you will, but carefully. Carefully remove the fish using a large spatula and drain on a paper towel–lined platter.

Transfer to a serving dish and serve with Spicy Lime and Chile Sauce.

NOTE: Aside from sea bass, other firm and meaty fish including red snapper, branzino, and tilapia are fantastic in this recipe. Ask your fishmonger what's freshest.

STINKY BEANS WITH SHRIMP

SATAW PAD GOONG

SERVES 2 TO 4

Every time my family takes a trip to the south, we all know *sataw*, or "stinky beans," is a must on Mom's to-do list. Despite the name, they're a delicacy. You'll see the twisted pods, about a foot long, piled up next to street vendors all across southern Thailand. Out of their pods, the bright green beans look like fava beans and, when cooked, have a similar nutty sweetness if also a certain distinct pungency. They're popular in Indonesian and Malaysian cooking as well, and are increasingly easy to find in the frozen section of large Asian markets. Here their earthiness pairs well with sweet fresh shrimp and the assertive flavors of chiles, garlic, and shrimp paste. If unavailable, tender spring asparagus can stand in for the stinky beans.

2 cloves garlic, roughly chopped

2 small fresh red Thai chiles, smashed

1 tablespoon vegetable oil

8 ounces large shrimp, peeled and deveined

2 cups fresh or thawed frozen shelled stinky beans (see Note)

1 tablespoon shrimp paste

Hot steamed jasmine or brown rice

In a stone mortar, combine the garlic and chiles and pound with a pestle to a coarse paste.

In a medium skillet, heat the oil over medium heat. Add the garlic and chile paste and stir until fragrant, about 1 minute. Add the shrimp and stir-fry for about 2 minutes, until the shrimp is cooked about halfway through. Add the stinky beans and toss for another minute. Add the shrimp paste and stir until the beans and shrimp are both cooked through, about 3 more minutes. The color of the beans will intensify from a light, grassy green to a beautiful, bright emerald as they cook. Serve with steamed jasmine or brown rice.

NOTE: If using fresh stinky beans, they must first be shelled like fava beans. Use a paring knife to cut each bean free from the large pod, take off the white or brown outer layer to reveal the bright, waxy green bean, and rinse. In the United States it's much more likely you'll find frozen stinky beans, even in specialty or Thai markets; for these just thaw them before adding them to the stir-fry.

ข้าวยำ

GRANDMA'S RICE BOWL

KHAO YUM

When my grandmother married my grandfather, they moved to southern Thailand, and my grandmother quickly mastered the art of southern Thai cooking. This is one of my family's most-loved dishes. I have fond memories of my mother and my aunts all working together in the kitchen, chopping the ingredients and making the dressing. Once it was ready, we all gathered together over our bowls of steamy rice with herbs and vegetables.

While it's true of many traditional Thai dishes, it's especially so of this one that proportions here are all guidelines and can—and should!—be tailored to your particular taste. Shredded green mango, ground dried shrimp, toasted coconut, and sliced wing beans are also popular additions to the dish. Prefer more coconut or kaffir lime? Use more! Don't want the heat from the chiles? Feel free to omit them.

FOR EACH PERSON

½ to 1 cup hot steamed jasmine or brown rice

2 tablespoons roughly chopped cucumber

¼ cup bean sprouts

¼ lime, very thinly sliced

2 kaffir lime leaves, thinly sliced

1 teaspoon thinly sliced lemongrass

¼ cup diced long beans

2 tablespoons Boodoo dressing (see Note), or to taste

3 betel leaves, thinly sliced (optional)

½ teaspoon red Thai chile powder, or to taste (optional)

Transfer the cooked rice to a large bowl while still hot. Gently fold in the remaining ingredients and serve hot.

NOTE: Boodoo dressing is a common Thai staple full of savory umami flavor. You can find it in Asian and specialty markets and online; if unavailable, a couple generous splashes of fish sauce will contribute a similar flavor.

กรุงเทพมหานคร

BANGKOK

BANGKOK

Deep-Fried Thai Pork Tartines
Khanom Bang Na Moo

Late-Night Rice Porridge
Khao Tom Rop Deuk

Son-in-Law Eggs
Khai Look Kheuy

Thai Scrambled Eggs
Khai Jiaw

Stuffed Cabbage Soup
Gaeng Jeud Galumplee Yad Sai

Green Papaya Salad
Som Tum

Three-Mushroom Salad
Yum Hed Sam Yang

Boat Noodles
Guay Tiaw Rua

Mah Mah Noodles with
Crabmeat and Chinese Broccoli
Mah Mah Pad Boo Gap Pak Kana

Stir-Fried Noodles
with Black Soy Sauce
Pad See Ew

Noodles and Gravy
Raad Na

Coconut Rice and Papaya Salad
Khao Mun Somtum

Rice with Shrimp Paste
Khao Khlug Grabi

Roasted Duck Curry
Gaeng Phet Bet Yang

Caramelized Pork Belly
Moo Wan

Crispy Catfish
with *Prik Khing* Sauce
Pla Dook Pad Prik Khing

Issan-Style *Shabu Shabu*
Jim Joom

Thaimee Fight Club Chicken
Gai Nung

Thai Ice Pops
Wan Yen

ขนมปังหน้าหมู

DEEP-FRIED THAI PORK TARTINES

KHANOM BANG NA MOO

MAKES 4

When I started dreaming about becoming a chef, this is one of the earliest dishes I mastered. Back then I was a career woman in limbo: Life was good but something was missing. In search of it, I found a new love, a new faith, and a new purpose. I realized I wanted to cook, serve, and share the love of good Thai food as I knew it. That's why this snack is dear to my heart. This fried bread filled with cilantro- and garlic-infused pork and served with refreshing cucumber relish brings back wonderful childhood memories of when I was a uniform-wearing schoolgirl riding the bus home at the end of the day to enjoy an afternoon snack.

3 cilantro roots, cleaned (or 1 bunch cilantro, finely chopped)

1 teaspoon freshly ground white pepper

1 clove garlic, cut into quarters

12 ounces ground pork

2 large eggs

3 tablespoons oyster sauce

4 slices white bread, left out to dry overnight and cut into 4 quarters

2 quarts vegetable oil

Salt

Cucumber Relish (page 226)

In a stone mortar, combine the cilantro roots, white pepper, and garlic and pound with a pestle into a coarse paste. Alternatively, process the ingredients in a food processor for about 2 minutes, until coarse. Transfer the paste to a large bowl and add the ground pork, eggs, and oyster sauce; mix well. Spread the pork mixture evenly onto the quartered bread slices.

Heat the oil in a deep-fryer or large saucepan to 375°F. Drop the pork-spread bread into the oil and fry until golden brown, about 3 minutes. Using a slotted spoon, transfer the tartines to a plate lined with paper towels and season with salt. Serve hot with Cucumber Relish.

ข้าวต้มรอบดึก

LATE-NIGHT RICE PORRIDGE

KHAO TOM ROP DEUK

SERVES 4

In Thailand you can find food around the clock, especially in Bangkok. *Khao tom kuy* is a kind of late-night restaurant in Thailand popular among the pub set, workaholics and partiers alike. These are some of my favorite dishes to order.

Pandan, *bai tooey*, is a popular culinary herb in Southeast Asia often added to dessert recipes, including cakes and porridges, or steeped in coconut milk. The long, slender green leaves (shown at left) have a nutty, floral fragrance. If not found fresh, frozen pandan leaves can be found in Asian markets—use them the same way as fresh.

3 quarts water

2 long fresh pandan leaves (optional)

1 cup uncooked jasmine rice

1 cup uncooked sticky rice

1 teaspoon salt

Traditional sides (recipes to follow on pages 130–31)

Combine the water with the lemongrass and pandan leaves, if using, in a large saucepan. Bring to a boil over high heat and add both types of rice. Cook, stirring often and adding water as needed, to prevent the rice from sticking to the bottom of the pan, for 15 to 20 minutes, until the rice has the consistency of a loose porridge. Remove from the heat and fluff lightly with a fork.

TO SERVE: Serve porridge with one or all of these traditional sides: Salted Egg Salad, Stir-Fried Bean Sprouts, *Kun Chiang* Sausage Salad, and Pickled Mustard Salad.

ยำไข่เค็ม

SALTED EGG SALAD

YUM KHAI KHEM

3 Salted Eggs (page 100)

2 to 3 fresh red Thai chiles, thinly sliced

1 small shallot, thinly sliced

2 tablespoons Simple Thai Salad Dressing
   (page 237)

2 sprigs cilantro, finely chopped

Quarter the salted eggs lengthwise and arrange on a small serving plate. Top with the chiles and shallot and drizzle with the salad dressing. Garnish with cilantro just before serving.

ผัดถั่วงอก

STIR-FRIED BEAN SPROUTS

PAD TAU NGOK

½ cup dried shiitake mushrooms

2 tablespoons vegetable oil

1 tablespoon smashed and chopped garlic

2 cups bean sprouts

1 cup cubed firm tofu (1-inch cubes)

1 scallion, cut into 2-inch pieces

1 fresh long red Thai chile, sliced diagonally
   ½ inch thick

1 tablespoon mushroom sauce, to taste

1 teaspoon ground white pepper

Soak the mushrooms in a bowl with warm water to cover until softened, 45 to 60 minutes. Remove the hydrated mushrooms with a fork and slice thinly. Discard the soaking liquid.

In a wok or a sauté pan, heat the oil over medium-high heat until sizzling. Add the garlic and sauté until fragrant, 1 to 2 minutes. Add the bean sprouts, tofu, mushrooms, scallion, and chile and cook, stirring, for another 2 minutes, until the bean sprouts are softened. Stir in the mushroom sauce. Transfer to a plate, sprinkle with the white pepper, and serve.

ยำกุนเชียง

KUN CHIANG SAUSAGE SALAD

YUM KUN CHIENG

1 cup *kun Chiang* or other Chinese dry sausage,
  cut into 1-inch pieces

1 small cucumber, quartered lengthwise and
  sliced ½ inch thick (about 1 cup)

½ cup thinly sliced onion

1 stalk Chinese celery, cut into 1-inch pieces
  (about ½ cup)

2 to 3 fresh red Thai chiles, to taste, finely chopped

2 tablespoons Simple Thai Salad Dressing
  (page 237)

Combine all the ingredients in a bowl and stir to combine well. Transfer to a plate and serve.

ยำเกี้ยมฉ่าย

PICKLED MUSTARD SALAD

YUM KIAM CHAI

1 cup chopped pickled mustard greens

2 to 3 fresh red Thai chiles, minced

1 shallot, thinly sliced

1 tablespoon Simple Thai Salad Dressing
  (page 237)

Combine all the ingredients in a bowl and stir to combine well. Transfer to a plate and serve.

SON-IN-LAW EGGS

KHAI LOOK KHEUY

SERVES 4

This recipe—eggs drizzled with a sweet and tangy sauce and topped with crispy shallots and fried chiles—is a dressed-up version of hard-boiled eggs. You're probably wondering why it's called son-in-law eggs. Well, Thais have a fondness for coming up with stories for food!

Here's the story behind this one: A man and his son-in-law planned to have a cook-off of *khai jiaw*, or Thai scrambled eggs, to show off to the women in their lives, the man's wife and daughter respectively. The father-in-law played a trick on the younger man by boiling all the eggs, so when it was the son-in-law's turn, he had no eggs! Not to be outdone, he got the idea to fry the boiled eggs and make a sweet and sour sauce along with some aromatic fried shallots and chiles. When they all sat down to dinner, the father-in-law teasingly asked the son how his eggs turned out, but the joke was on him, because the son-in-law's eggs were the favorite.

FOR THE SAUCE

1 cup tamarind concentrate

½ cup shaved palm sugar

½ cup fish sauce

FOR THE FRIED SHALLOTS AND CHILES

½ cup vegetable oil

½ cup thinly sliced shallots

3 or 4 whole dried red Thai chiles

FOR THE EGGS

2 quarts vegetable oil

4 hard-boiled eggs, peeled

¼ cup roughly chopped cilantro

Hot steamed jasmine or brown rice

TO PREPARE THE SAUCE: In a small saucepan, combine the tamarind concentrate, sugar, and fish sauce, place over medium heat, and cook, stirring, for about 10 minutes, until the sugar is dissolved and the sauce starts to thicken. Remove from the heat and set aside.

TO PREPARE THE FRIED SHALLOTS AND CHILES: In a medium saucepan, heat the oil over low heat. Add the shallots and fry until golden, about 5 minutes. Using a slotted spoon, remove the shallots from the oil and set aside on a paper towel–lined plate. Add the chiles to the same oil and fry until they crisp up and their color darkens, about 2 minutes. Using a slotted spoon, remove the chiles from the oil and set aside on another paper towel–lined plate. Discard the oil.

TO FRY THE EGGS: In a wok or a deep sauce-pan, heat the vegetable oil over medium heat to 375°F. Carefully lower the boiled eggs into the oil and fry until golden brown, 3 to 4 minutes. Remove the eggs from the oil using the slotted spoon to a paper towel–lined plate to drain and cool.

TO SERVE: Cut the eggs in half and divide them among plates. Pour the sauce over the eggs and top with the fried shallots, whole fried chiles, and cilantro. Serve with steamed jasmine or brown rice.

ไข่เจียว

THAI SCRAMBLED EGGS

KHAI JIAW

SERVES 1

This is the quintessential Thai comfort food: hot, crispy, fluffy eggs over a plate of steamy jasmine rice with Fish Sauce with Chiles (page 226). Ask any of your Thai friends and they will likely tell you how much they love this dish.

2 tablespoons vegetable oil

2 eggs

1 shallot, thinly sliced

2 to 3 ounces ground pork, ground shrimp, or lump crabmeat; or 1 cup chopped Thai basil leaves (optional)

Hor steamed jasmine rice

1 teaspoon Fish Sauce with Chiles (see page 226), or mushroom sauce if vegetarian

Sriracha sauce (optional)

Heat the oil in a medium skillet or wok over medium-heat high.

In a small bowl, beat the eggs until light and fluffy. Add the shallot, fish sauce, and any other ingredients you like.

Once the oil is smoking hot, pour the egg mixture into the skillet and cook for about 2 minutes to set, then flip and cook for another 2 to 3 minutes, a little longer if you are using pork, shrimp, crab, or basil leaves, until just cooked through.

Serve on a bed of steamed jasmine rice. Season with Fish Sauce with Chiles and/or Sriracha sauce if you want more heat.

แกงจืดกะหล่ำปลียัดไส้

STUFFED CABBAGE SOUP

GAENG JEUD GALUMPLEE YAD SAI

SERVES 4 TO 6

Another great cook in my family is my aunt Aoy. She lives in Bangkok, and every time I visit her, I can count on having a fantastic homemade meal (or many!). My favorite dish from her kitchen is a soup of pork-stuffed cabbage. Aunt Aoy marinates the ground pork with cilantro root, garlic, and white pepper before carefully tucking it between layers of market-fresh cabbage. To me, this cooked cabbage—and its rich, flavorful broth—is the best kind of comfort food.

1 pound ground pork

1 tablespoon finely chopped cilantro root

1 tablespoon finely chopped garlic

2 teaspoons freshly ground white pepper

2 tablespoons oyster sauce

1 cup dried oyster mushrooms

6 cups Thai Chicken Stock (page 236)

1 medium green cabbage, cored and quartered

2 tablespoons mushroom sauce, or to taste

In a medium bowl, combine the pork, cilantro root, garlic, white pepper, and oyster sauce until the ingredients are well incorporated. Cover and refrigerate to marinate for 20 minutes.

In a small bowl, cover the dried mushrooms in warm water and leave for 20 minutes to soften. Drain the mushrooms, place on a paper towel, and discard the soaking liquid.

In a large saucepan, bring the stock to a boil over high heat. Meanwhile, take the pork mixture and stuff it evenly between 3 or 4 layers of the quartered cabbage like a lasagna. Once the stock comes to a boil, add the stuffed quartered cabbage to the pot, cut side down, then add the mushrooms. Cover, reduce the heat to medium-low, and simmer for about 45 minutes, until the cabbage is cooked through. Remove from the heat and season with mushroom sauce. Spoon into bowls and serve.

ส้มตำ

GREEN PAPAYA SALAD

SOM TUM

SERVES 2 TO 4

There's a special place in the hearts of all Thai people for *som tum*, or papaya salad. There's something about the sour-and-spicy flavor combination that excites Thai taste buds—but the salad also has a healing effect. Throughout college, my buddies and I would always go to the same shack near our school to talk about boys and eat our *som tum*, slurping up the shredded papaya dressed in savory *pla la* sauce and sweating and sometimes tearing up from the spiciness. We would laugh together and wonder why we were doing this to ourselves, whether it was waiting for that one boy we knew wouldn't call back or suffering the heat of the Thai chiles. But in the end we always walked away satisfied, and many broken hearts were healed during our *som tum* ritual. *Som tum* is the perfect therapy session.

2 tablespoons palm sugar

2 tablespoons tamarind concentrate

2 teaspoons lime juice

2 tablespoons fish sauce
(or mushroom sauce if vegetarian)

Pla la (optional; see Note)

3 small cloves garlic

1 to 2 fresh red Thai chiles, to taste

1 green papaya, peeled and shredded
(about 2 cups)

½ cup cherry tomatoes, quartered

½ cup long beans cut into 2-inch pieces

2 tablespoons roasted peanuts

Dried shrimp (optional)

In a small saucepan, combine the sugar, tamarind concentrate, lime juice, fish sauce, and *pla la*, if using, to taste, and stir over medium heat just until the sugar is dissolved and the flavors mix. Remove from the heat and set aside to cool.

In a mortar, combine the garlic and chiles and pound with a pestle until they release their oils and break down, 3 to 4 minutes. Be careful not to completely crush them. Add the papaya and continue to pound, about 1 minute, until the papaya is softened but not pulverized. Add the tomatoes and long beans, pounding in between additions to soften the vegetables. (It may seem like this will yield a bowl of mush, but green papaya has a crunchy texture that holds up to the mortar and pestle.)

Drizzle the cooled dressing over the pounded vegetables and, using the pestle, gently mix. Serve on plates topped with roasted peanuts and dried shrimp, if desired.

NOTE: Like Boodoo dressing (see page 120), *pla la* sauce is a tangy fermented fish–based condiment popular throughout Thailand. If you can't find it in Asian markets or online, a couple of extra splashes of fish sauce, *nam pla*, will contribute a similar salty flavor.

ยำเห็ดสามอย่าง

THREE-MUSHROOM SALAD

YUM HED SAM YANG

SERVES 4

My whole life my mom has been telling me that eating a mix of three mushrooms has a detoxifying effect. Her advice inspired me to create a dish that is healthy, full of flavor, and great for entertaining my vegetarian friends! This is my favorite combination of mushrooms, but feel free to experiment with what looks good at your local farmers' or foragers' market. For extra crunch, top the salad with some toasted peanuts or cashews.

1 teaspoon salt

1 cup sliced king oyster mushrooms (¼- to ½-inch-thick coins)

1 cup hen-of-the-woods mushrooms

1 cup enoki mushrooms

¼ cup Simple Thai Salad Dressing (page 237)

1 small shallot, very thinly sliced into rounds

½ cup chopped Chinese celery (1-inch pieces)

2 tablespoons coarsely chopped cilantro leaves

Prepare an ice water bath.

In a large saucepan, bring 2 quarts water to a boil over high heat. Add the salt, then add the king oyster and hen-of-the-woods mushrooms and cook until just softened, about 3 minutes. Add the enoki mushrooms and stir for 1 minute more.

Using a slotted spoon, remove the cooked mushrooms from the pan to the ice water bath to cool, then drain and transfer to a medium bowl. Add the dressing, shallot, Chinese celery, and cilantro and toss.

ก๋วยเตี๋ยวเรือ

BOAT NOODLES

GUAY TIAW RUA

SERVES 4

It's a little-known fact that Bangkok was once called the Venice of the East. During the nineteenth century, the city was home to a system of expansive canals (called *klongs*) that connected houses, temples, and public spaces. Boating was the most common form of transportation for both people and commerce. At one point, there were more floating markets than land-based ones! Bangkok's transport system shifted to roads at the turn of the twentieth century, but some of the foods that originated within the canal lifestyle have survived.

Perhaps the most famous of these is boat noodles, a small but rich pho-like dish served with fresh bean sprouts, Thai basil, crispy pork skin, and a row of condiments. Two Bangkok neighborhoods are synonymous with boat noodles: Rangsit and Anutsaovaree Chaisamorapoom (aka Victory Monument).

My very favorite version to order is *woonsen moo chin sod tok perm nam perm pak*. My former teachers would not approve of that sloppy Thai grammar, but that's how we say it at the noodle stalls! It means, "I'll have vermicelli noodles with pork, pork ball, extra-bloody broth, and extra vegetables." It should come as no surprise that a noodle lover like me would leave a stack of bowls behind on the table!

2 quarts Pork Stock (page 236)

½ cup pork blood (optional, but traditional)

4 tablespoons Thai Chiles in Vinegar (page 225)

8 teaspoons sugar

4 tablespoons fish sauce

1 pound rice stick noodles (or any noodles of your choice, such as wheat vermicelli noodles, rice vermicelli noodles, wide rice noodles, or *mah mah* noodles), hydrated in room-temperature water until tender or following the package instructions

1 pound pork tenderloin, thinly sliced

1 cup store-bought pork meatballs

1 quart bean sprouts

4 cups water spinach cut into 2-inch pieces

4 tablespoons Fried Garlic (page 231)

½ cup crispy pork skin

½ cup roughly chopped scallions

½ cup roughly chopped cilantro

½ cup roughly chopped Chinese celery

Freshly ground white pepper

In a large saucepan, bring the stock to a boil over high heat. Lower the heat to maintain a simmer and add the pork blood, if using.

Ready four individual soup bowls and add 1 tablespoon chiles in vinegar, 2 teaspoons sugar, and 1 tablespoon fish sauce to each.

In a large saucepan, bring 4 quarts water to a boil and set the pan up with a blanching basket or steamer insert. Blanch the tenderloin and meatballs in the boiling water for 3 to 5 minutes, just until the tenderloin is no longer pink and the meatballs are hot, then divide among the four prepared bowls. Repeat with the noodles for 2 to 3 minutes, just until tender, and the bean sprouts and water spinach, just until wilted, and divide these among the bowls.

Ladle hot stock over the noodles in each bowl. Season with fried garlic, crispy pork skin, scallions, cilantro, Chinese celery, and white pepper to taste and serve.

NOTES: This recipe is a *nam tok* broth, which means it contains blood. But if bloody broth is too adventurous for you, you can try it without. In that case, this bowl of noodles would be called *nam sai*. You can make the same recipe with beef if you are not a pork eater.

มาม่าผัดปูกับผักคะน้า

MAH MAH NOODLES WITH CRABMEAT AND CHINESE BROCCOLI

MAH MAH PAD BOO GAP PAK KANA

SERVES 4

Mah mah is a kind of instant noodle that is so ubiquitous in Thailand that its name is now synonymous with "instant noodle" in Thai. In some circles, it is looked down upon, but it holds an important place in my heart (and I'm sure many other Thais would say the same). When I was in elementary school, I always bought myself a pack while waiting for the bus to school for 2 baht or so (less than 1 cent), crushing the noodles into small crunchy, delicious pieces. Decades later, as a career woman in Bangkok, I made my own version of this dish: The result is a grown-up version of a kid's dream.

2 (4.2-ounce) packages instant noodles

2 tablespoons vegetable oil

1 teaspoon minced garlic

2 eggs

2 whole jumbo Maryland blue crabs, cleaned, shelled, and cut into 4 pieces each

1 cup chopped Chinese broccoli or kale leaves

1 carrot, cut into thin julienne

2 tablespoons oyster sauce

6 ounces fresh lump crabmeat (about ½ cup)

Lime wedges

Four classic Thai condiments (page 225)

Cook the instant noodles according to the package directions to al dente. Drain, rinse well under cold water, and set aside.

In a wok or wide sauté pan, heat the oil over medium-high heat. Add the garlic and cook, stirring, until aromatic, about 1 minute, taking care not to let it burn. Crack the eggs into the wok and using a wooden spatula, break the yolks and stir, and raise the heat to high. Add the crab, Chinese broccoli, carrot, and oyster sauce. Cook, stirring occasionally, until cooked through, 4 to 5 minutes. Add the cooked noodles and crabmeat and fold them in gently to avoid breaking up the crabmeat.

Serve with lime wedges and the four classic Thai condiments.

ผัดซีอิ๊ว

STIR-FRIED NOODLES WITH BLACK SOY SAUCE

PAD SEE EW

SERVES 4

Pad means "to stir-fry," and *see ew* is the name of the sauce in this popular Chinese-influenced dish. Everything else—the noodles, protein, and vegetables—is up to you! And don't be stingy with the heat—the key to a great stir-fried dish is high heat, especially when you're looking for that smoky-sweet wok-charred flavor.

2 tablespoons vegetable oil

1 teaspoon finely chopped garlic

2 eggs

8 ounces protein, such as thinly sliced boneless chicken breast or thighs, thinly sliced pork or beef tenderloin, peeled and deveined medium shrimp, calamari rings, or diced firm tofu

2 cups cooked wide rice noodles, or noodle of your choice

3 tablespoons See Ew Sauce (recipe follows)

1 cup Chinese broccoli or kale leaves cut into strips

1 cup thinly sliced carrots, broccoli or cauliflower florets, or halved Brussels sprouts, blanched (optional)

1 cup bean sprouts (optional)

1 teaspoon freshly ground white pepper

Lime wedges

Four classic Thai condiments (page 225)

In a wok or wide sauté pan, heat the oil with the garlic over medium-high heat and stir until aromatic, about 1 minute. Working quickly, add the eggs and use a wooden spatula to break the yolks and stir, about 1 minute. Raise the heat to high, add the protein, and cook, stirring, until the protein is almost cooked through, 1 to 2 minutes. Add the noodles and sauce and stir to coat. Add the vegetables and cook, stirring, until just cooked, about 3 minutes. Remove from the heat and stir in the bean sprouts and white pepper. Serve with lime wedges and the four classic Thai condiments.

NOTE: When working with high heat, you want to expedite the process as much as possible, and blanching hardy vegetables ahead of time for a minute or so in just-boiling water helps keep things moving. Just be sure to drain them well; you don't want to add wet vegetables to your stir-fry. You won't burn your dish if you keep a close eye on things and move quickly.

SEE EW SAUCE

MAKES 1 CUP

¼ cup oyster sauce

¼ cup mushroom sauce

½ cup black sweet soy sauce

2 tablespoons sugar

Combine all the ingredients in a small saucepan, place over medium heat, and stir until the sugar dissolves, about 5 minutes. Remove from heat and let cool.

Keep refrigerated in an airtight container for up to 3 months.

ราดหน้า

NOODLES AND GRAVY

RAAD NA

SERVES 4

This is the twin dish of *pad see ew*. Between you and me, this one's my favorite.

Raad na means "to pour something on top," and this dish is all about the gravy that you pour over the cooked noodles. As with *pad see ew*, you can choose your favorite noodles and protein. As for me, I prefer *sen mee raad na moo sai pak yur yur*—rice vermicelli noodles with pork and extra vegetables.

½ cup dried shiitake mushrooms (optional)

1 pound pork tenderloin, thinly sliced (or substitute chicken, shrimp, beef, calamari, or firm tofu)

3 tablespoons oyster sauce

3 tablespoons cornstarch

3 tablespoons vegetable oil

2 tablespoons black soy sauce

2 cups soft flat rice noodles (see Note)

2 teaspoons minced garlic

2 cups chopped Chinese broccoli or kale leaves

1 medium carrot, sliced into thin coins

1 quart Thai Chicken Stock (page 236) or water

¼ cup Thai miso, or to taste

2 tablespoons mushroom sauce

1 tablespoon sugar

½ teaspoon freshly ground white pepper

Four classic Thai condiments (page 225)

If using the mushrooms, soak them in a bowl with warm water to cover until softened, 45 to 60 minutes. Remove the mushrooms with a fork, pat dry, and discard the soaking liquid. You can use the mushrooms whole, halved, or quartered, as preferred.

Place the pork in a large bowl. Toss with 2 tablespoons of the oyster sauce to coat well and leave on the counter to marinate for 30 minutes.

In a small bowl, whisk the cornstarch into ½ cup room-temperature water.

Heat a wok or wide sauté pan over medium heat. Quickly add 1 tablespoon of the vegetable oil, the black soy sauce, and the noodles and toss until well coated. Transfer to a plate and set aside.

In the same wok, add the remaining 2 tablespoons oil and raise the heat to medium-high. Add the garlic and

stir until fragrant, about 1 minute, watching carefully so it doesn't burn. Add the marinated pork and cook, stirring often, until partially cooked, about 5 minutes.

Add the Chinese broccoli and carrot and cook for another 3 to 4 minutes, until both the pork and vegetables are cooked.

Add the stock and bring to a simmer. Add the cornstarch mixture and stir well, returning the stock to a simmer. Season with the Thai miso and stir in the mushroom sauce, sugar, and the remaining oyster sauce.

Transfer to a serving bowl and serve topped with the white pepper and the four classic Thai condiments.

NOTE: The noodles for *raad na* and *pad see ew* (page 148) are bought soft and recipe-ready, no hydrating required.

ข้าวมันส้มตำ

COCONUT RICE AND PAPAYA SALAD

KHAO MUN SOMTUM

SERVES 4

These classic dishes trace their origins back to the court of King Rama V, but whether prepared in the royal palace or your family's kitchen, they're special additions to any meal. In Thailand you can find many varieties of *som tum*, and at Ngam I often use berries, chopped apple or pear, or even grilled watermelon in place of the traditional cherry tomatoes and long beans—the sweet, seasonal fruit making a delicious contrast to the spicy, tangy dressing.

FOR THE COCONUT RICE

1½ cups jasmine rice

3 cups coconut milk

¼ cup sugar

2 teaspoons salt

¼ cup toasted dried unsweetened
   shredded coconut

FOR THE PAPAYA SALAD

3 small cloves garlic

1 to 2 fresh red Thai chiles, or to taste

2 cups shredded fresh green papaya

1 cup chopped seasonal fruit, such as strawberries,
   apples, or melon

1 tablespoon palm sugar

1 tablespoon tamarind concentrate

2 teaspoons fresh lime juice, or 1 lime wedge

1 tablespoon fish sauce

2 tablespoons roasted peanuts

¼ cup dried shrimp

TO MAKE THE COCONUT RICE: Rinse the rice well and set aside.

Combine the coconut milk, sugar, and salt in a medium saucepan. Place over low heat and stir until dissolved. Stir in the rice, increase the heat to high, and bring to a boil, stirring occasionally. Reduce the heat to low, cover, and simmer for about 20 minutes, until the rice absorbs all the coconut milk mixture. Spoon into a serving bowl and top with toasted coconut.

WHILE THE RICE IS COOKING, MAKE THE PAPAYA SALAD: In a stone mortar, combine the garlic and chiles and pound with a pestle until they release their oils and break down, about 1 minute. Be careful not to completely crush them. Add the green papaya and continue to pound for about 1 minute, until the papaya is bruised and softened but not pulverized. Repeat with the chopped fruit, pounding lightly to soften. Add the sugar, tamarind concentrate, lime juice or wedge, and fish sauce and gently mix with the mortar. Transfer to plates and top with the peanuts and dried shrimp.

Serve the papaya salad and coconut rice family-style alongside hearty braises or curries or as part of a large menu.

ข้าวคลุกกะปิ

RICE WITH SHRIMP PASTE

KHAO KHLUG GRABI

SERVES 4 TO 6

This dish—rice mixed with shrimp paste and topped with dried shrimp, fresh green mango, Thai chiles, thinly sliced scrambled eggs, and caramelized pork—is a Thai delicacy, with a new flavor in every bite. Don't let the list of ingredients or the less than exciting name turn you away from trying it—this dish is full of adventurous flavors and is simpler than it looks. I guarantee you will fall in love with it!

FOR THE EGG CREPE

1 tablespoon vegetable oil

2 eggs

FOR THE RICE

2 tablespoons vegetable oil

2 cloves garlic, chopped

2 cups steamed jasmine rice

1/4 cup shrimp paste

FOR THE TOPPINGS

1/2 cup dried shrimp

1/4 cup thinly sliced shallots

2 fresh red Thai chiles, thinly sliced, or to taste

Caramelized Pork Belly (page 158)

1/2 cup julienned green mango

1/2 cup thinly sliced long beans

TO MAKE THE EGG CREPE: Heat the oil in a small nonstick skillet over medium-low heat. In a small bowl, beat the eggs. Spread the eggs out so that they form a crepelike layer in the bottom of the pan and cook, stirring gently, until the egg is just set, 2 to 3 minutes. Using a spatula, transfer the egg crepe to a cutting board. Cool completely, about 5 minutes, then roll the crepe like a cigar, cut into 1/2-inch strips, and set aside.

TO MAKE THE RICE: In a wok or a sauté pan, heat the oil over medium-high heat. Add the garlic and sauté, stirring, for about 2 minutes, until golden and fragrant. Add the rice and shrimp paste and stir with a wooden spatula until heated through. Remove from the heat and set aside.

TO ASSEMBLE: Put a scoop of rice in the center of each bowl with a small serving of each of the toppings around it. Top with the sliced egg crepe.

แกงเผ็ดเป็ดย่าง

ROASTED DUCK CURRY

GAENG PHET BET YANG

SERVES 4

Working and living in Bangkok introduced me to many new curry dishes. This recipe is one of my favorites because it's both simple and full of refreshing flavors and the combination of duck and red curry sings alongside the fresh fruit and aromatic herbs.

Living in New York City, this comforting red curry full of the Thai flavors I crave is easy to make, facilitated by the perfectly roasted duck I can get from my favorite place in Chinatown anytime I like. Diced pineapple or seedless grapes can make good, sweet stand-ins for the lychees.

FOR THE DUCK

2 tablespoons black soy sauce

2 tablespoons mushroom sauce

2 tablespoons light brown sugar

2 teaspoons vegetable oil

½ duck, both leg and breast (12 to 16 ounces)

FOR THE CURRY

1 (13.5-ounce) can coconut milk

1 cup Red Curry Paste (page 229)

½ cup lychees (canned or fresh, peeled and pitted)

½ cup cherry tomato halves

1 fresh long red Thai chile, thinly sliced

1 cup whole Thai basil leaves

2 tablespoons fish sauce

2 tablespoons palm sugar

Hot steamed jasmine or brown rice

ROAST THE DUCK: Preheat the oven to 375°F.

In a large bowl, whisk together the black soy sauce, mushroom sauce, brown sugar, and oil to make a marinade. Add the duck and marinate for 30 minutes on the counter or up to overnight in the refrigerator.

Remove the duck from the marinade. Place the duck on a roasting pan skin-side up, place in the oven, and roast for about 25 minutes, until the internal temperature reads 175°F at the joints and leg. Remove from the oven and let rest for 5 minutes, then remove the leg and thigh and slice the breast.

MAKE THE CURRY: Skim 2 tablespoons of coconut cream from the can. Add to a small saucepan and whisk in the curry paste. Place over medium heat and stir just until the color of the paste deepens, about 2 minutes.

Add the duck and the remaining coconut milk, bring to a simmer, and simmer for about 5 minutes, until the curry thickens. Add the lychees, tomatoes, chile, and Thai basil and cook, stirring, just until the herbs wilt, another 2 to 3 minutes. Add the fish sauce and sugar and remove from the heat.

Serve hot with steamed jasmine or brown rice.

หมูหวาน

CARAMELIZED PORK BELLY

MOO WAN

SERVES 4

The name of this dish literally translates to "sweet pork." The authentic technique for making it is to caramelize palm sugar before stirring in the pork belly and cooking it until it's almost candied. I find *moo wan* to be the best condiment for a very old-school Thai dish called *kao klug krabi* (Rice with Shrimp Paste; page 155), and it also makes for a delicious sandwich—think Thai-style pulled pork, but stickier.

¼ cup vegetable oil

3 to 4 shallots, thinly sliced

2 tablespoons minced garlic

1 cup palm sugar

2 pounds pork belly, cut into 1-inch chunks

About 1½ cups water

¼ cup mushroom sauce

2 tablespoons black soy sauce

Salt

Hot steamed jasmine or brown rice

Heat the oil in a medium sauté pan over medium heat. Add the shallots and garlic and cook, stirring, until fragrant, about 2 minutes. Add the sugar and continue stirring until the sugar is dissolved and caramelized into a dark amber color, about 10 minutes. Add the pork belly and mix well.

Add just enough water to cover the pork, then add the mushroom sauce, black soy sauce, and salt to taste. Bring to a boil, then lower the heat to medium-low and simmer for about 40 minutes, stirring occasionally, until the pork is very soft, almost falling apart, and the sauce is thickened to the consistency of a glaze. Serve over steamed jasmine or brown rice.

ปลาดุกผัดพริกขิง

CRISPY CATFISH WITH *PRIK KHING* SAUCE

PLA DOOK PAD PRIK KHING

SERVES 2 TO 4

Kao rad kang, or curry over rice, is an undeniable part of Thai food culture. When I was working in Bangkok, it was the most popular lunch among my coworkers. We'd each order a different dish from the street food carts and all share, and this was my favorite. Truthfully, it was more bonding than any team-building workshop!

2 quarts vegetable oil

¼ cup Thai holy basil leaves (if you can't find Thai holy basil, regular Thai basil will do)

Salt

1 pound catfish (about 6 small fillets)

½ cup *Prik Khing* Curry Paste (page 230)

2 fresh long red Thai chiles, sliced diagonally ¼ inch thick

¼ cup julienned krachai

5 kaffir lime leaves, torn and cut into thin chiffonade (reserve some for garnish)

1 teaspoon fish sauce

1 teaspoon palm sugar

Hot steamed jasmine or brown rice

2 Salted Eggs (page 100; optional)

In a wok or large saucepan, heat the oil to 375°F (or until it makes a crackling noise when you put a small piece of basil in the oil) over medium-high heat. Add the Thai holy basil and fry until crispy, about 2 minutes. Spoon the basil out with a slotted spoon and set aside on a baking sheet lined with paper towels. Season with salt.

Add the catfish fillets to the oil and fry until golden brown, about 7 minutes. Remove from the oil using a slotted spoon and set aside on the prepared baking sheet.

In a wok or a large skillet, heat about 2 tablespoons oil from frying the fish over medium-high heat. Add the curry paste and heat until fragrant, about 2 minutes, stirring to avoid browning the paste. Add the fried catfish, the chiles, krachai, kaffir lime leaves, fish sauce, and sugar. Remove from the heat. Serve over rice and garnish with the reserved kaffir lime leaves and the fried Thai holy basil. Crumble the salted eggs on top, if using, or serve them alongside.

ISSAN-STYLE *SHABU SHABU*

JIM JOOM

SERVES 4 TO 6

I am a sucker for *shabu shabu*, also known as hot pot. It's originally from northeastern Thailand, which means it's going to be a little spicy and sour, or what we call *zab*! I love everything about it—the communal way of eating (the more the merrier!), the fresh ingredients, the savory broth, and the tangy dipping sauce. Whenever I get together with friends, this is my go-to recipe. What's better than good food with good company?

Jim means to dip into a sauce, and *joom* means to dip into water. In this case, the protein and vegetables will be dipped into a boiling hot broth to cook and then into a dipping sauce. The key to good hot pot is a killer broth and dipping sauces—Issan-Style Dipping Sauce and Spicy Lime and Chile Sauce and everything else can be tailored to your taste—try it also with lobster or tofu.

Shabu shabu is a party dish, where everyone participates in making and enjoying the food. Set the broth in a large, heavy pot on a hot plate, portable burner, or even a slow cooker in the center of the table. *(See following pages.)*

FOR THE BROTH

4 quarts Thai Chicken Stock (page 236)

4 stalks lemongrass, cut into 2- to 3-inch pieces, bruised

1 Chinese radish, peeled and cut into 2-inch cubes, about 1 cup

1 cup whole Thai basil leaves

2 to 3 small shallots, peeled and bruised

2 to 3 fresh or dried red Thai chiles

FOR THE *SHABU SHABU*

1 head Napa cabbage, leaves separated

5 scallions, cut into 1- to 2-inch lengths

1 pound water spinach or baby spinach leaves

2 cups whole Thai basil leaves, torn

8 ounces vermicelli noodles, soaked in room-temperature water until softened, about 30 minutes

1 pound medium shrimp, peeled and deveined

1 pound calamari, cut into rings

1 pound beef tenderloin, thinly sliced

1 pound pork tenderloin, thinly sliced

1 pound mushrooms of your choice, such as oyster or enoki

4 eggs

2 limes, cut into wedges

Issan-Style Dipping Sauce (page 234)

Spicy Lime and Chile Sauce (page 235)

Distribute the cabbage, scallions, water spinach, basil, noodles, shrimp, calamari, meat, mushrooms, and eggs in small dishes around the table. Everyone should have utensils (long chopsticks are traditional), a small soup bowl or plate, and a soupspoon.

Now, party! Place a hot plate in the center of the table. In a large pot, bring the stock, lemongrass, radish, basil, shallots, and chiles to a gentle boil. Everyone can take turns adding torn cabbage leaves, scallions, water spinach, Thai basil, and mushrooms to the broth, then stir in some noodles.

Dip or drop shrimp, calamari, pork, and beef into the broth just long enough to cook it to desired doneness.

The eggs can be either cracked into the broth and stirred to create thin ribbons or poached whole in the broth.

As a communal dish, it's fun to all create one pot together, but you can also pour the hot broth into soup bowls for individual portions.

Season individual portions with squeezes of lime (you don't want to add lime to the bubbling broth, as boiling lime juice can make it bitter), with the dipping sauces alongside.

NOTE: Chopsticks came to Thailand from the Chinese, and are used almost exclusively with noodle dishes and soups, such as this hot pot. Most dishes, including rice, are eaten with a fork and spoon. Very traditional northern and northeastern Thai dishes are usually eaten with pinches of sticky rice and clean hands.

ไก่นึ่ง

THAIMEE FIGHT CLUB CHICKEN

GAI NUNG

SERVES 4 TO 6

Thai boxing is my new love. It's so much fun, and I sweat like crazy! My friends tease me that I will start my own fight club one day. I first discovered this dish at my friend's restaurant in Bangkok and fell in love with it. I can't get over the punch of flavors from the juicy farm-raised chicken and the aromatic broth of lemongrass and lemon basil. Not only that, but it's super easy to make and packed with protein. Welcome to Thaimee Fight Club!

1 whole farm-raised chicken (about 3 pounds), cut into 8 bone-in pieces

1 cup Ngam's House Marinade (page 227)

1 (2-inch) piece galangal, sliced into 5 or 6 pieces

3 pieces lemongrass, bruised and cut into 3- to 4-inch pieces

6 kaffir lime leaves, torn into quarters

3 cilantro roots, cleaned and bruised (or 3 whole bunches fresh cilantro, chopped)

¼ cup whole lemon basil leaves

Hot steamed sticky rice

In a large bowl, rub the chicken all over with the marinade, cover, and let marinate in the refrigerator for at least 30 minutes or up to overnight.

Prepare a large double boiler. You're going to be steaming the chicken pieces, but you don't want to lose the juices through a basket insert with holes. In a pinch, you can use a bowl that fits inside a tall pot, but don't let the bottom of the bowl touch the simmering water.

Place the marinated chicken pieces in the steamer and add the galangal, lemongrass, kaffir lime leaves, cilantro roots, and lemon basil. Steam until fully cooked, when an instant-read thermometer reads 160°F when inserted into a thigh. For large bone-in pieces this could take as long as 1 hour, so monitor the meat and water level carefully.

Remove from the heat. Transfer to a shallow bowl and serve hot with sticky rice, passing the juices from the chicken separately.

หวานเย็น

THAI ICE POPS

WAN YEN

MAKES ABOUT 10 POPS, DEPENDING ON MOLD

Thailand's hot, humid climate and abundance of tropical fruit come together deliciously in a variety of frozen treats, including handcrafted popsicles flavored with coconut water, fruit juice, or tamarind. The liquid is poured into metal molds submerged in a bath of ice water and rock salt, and agitated or shaken to flash-freeze. A popular, portable treat often found in markets and on the street, any of these recipes can also be made at home in popsicle molds that go into the freezer—experiment with any combination below or try it with Thai Iced Tea (page 177).

Pour the chilled mixture into ice pop molds and freeze until solid, 5 to 6 hours or overnight. For a slushier, granita-type texture, pour the chilled mixture into a baking dish and freeze, scraping with a fork every 20 to 30 minutes for about 1½ hours, until fluffy and set.

THAI ICED TEA

1 quart water

2 cups Thai tea powder

1 cup granulated sugar

1 cup sweetened condensed milk

In a large saucepan, bring the water to a simmer over medium heat. Add the tea powder and sugar and stir until dissolved, about 5 minutes. Remove from the heat, add the condensed milk, and let cool completely.

STRAWBERRY AND LYCHEE

1 pint strawberries, hulled

1 (20-ounce) can lychees in syrup

½ teaspoon jasmine extract

In a blender, combine all the ingredients and blend until smooth.

HONEYDEW AND COCONUT

1 (13.5-ounce) can coconut milk

¼ cup palm sugar, or to taste

¼ medium honeydew, peeled, seeded and cut into chunks (about 2 cups)

In a medium saucepan, combine the coconut milk and sugar. Place over low heat and heat, stirring, for about 5 minutes, until the sugar is dissolved. Remove from the heat and let cool completely. Transfer to a blender, add the honeydew, and blend until smooth.

PASSION FRUIT AND CHILE

2 cups passion fruit concentrate

1 fresh red Thai chile

2 cups water

Sea salt

In a blender, combine the passion fruit concentrate and chile and blend until smooth. Transfer to a pitcher and stir in the water. Sprinkle with the salt when serving.

มหานครนิวยอร์ค

NEW YORK CITY

Modern Thai
Comfort Food

มหานครนิวยอร์ค
NEW YORK CITY

Fresh Fruit Shake
Nam Polamai Pun

Thai Soda
Nam Soda

Thai Iced Tea
Cha Yen

Ngam House Cocktails

Chiang Mai Fries
Krah Bong

Oyster Shooters with
Spicy Lime and Chile Sauce
Hoi Nang Rom Shot

Spring Rolls
Baw Bia

Sweet Corn Fritters
with Cucumber Relish
Tod Mun Khao Pote Gap Ajard

The 15-Minute Soup
That Changed My Life
Tom Khlong

Rustic Chicken Soup
Yum Jin Gai

Thai Corn Chowder
Soup Khao Pote

Spicy Kale and Mushroom Salad
Yum Kale Kub Het

Chiang Mai–Inspired Salmon
Tiratido
Saa Salmon

Thai Garden Salad with
Miang Dressing
Yum Miang Kham

Old-School *Pad Thai*
with Shrimp
Pad Thai

Papaya or Zucchini *Pad Thai*
with Shrimp
Pad Thai Malako,
Pad Thai Zucchini Goong Sot

The Dark Knight
Sen Muek Dam Pad Prik Thai
Dam Kub Pla Muek Krob

Grilled Chicken
Gai Yang

Happy Tiger
Sua Dee Jai

My Thai Burger
Sai Ooa Burger

Spicy Steamed Bass with Ginger
Pla Nueng Khing Gub Nam
Jim Talay

Green Curry Fried Rice
Khao Pad Gaeng Khiaw Wan

Kale Fried Rice
Khao Pad Kale

Pumpkin and Thai Basil
Fak Tong Pad Khai Sai Horapa

Thai Red Curry Pumpkin Pie
Pie Fak Tong

Thai Tea–Poached Pears
Look Pear Chuam Chayen

น้ำผลไม้ปั่น

FRESH FRUIT SHAKE

NAM POLAMAI PUN

SERVES 1

I feel blessed to have grown up in a country with an abundance of amazing fruits. And because it's a tropical country, we would eat them fresh all year round. I prefer to use honey as sweetener in these fruit shakes, but you may also use agave nectar or simple syrup or omit the sugar altogether. Elevate any of these into an adult version by adding a splash of vodka, sake, or *soju*.

HONEYDEW

1 cup chopped honeydew

1 cup ice

⅓ cup coconut milk

1 tablespoon honey, or to taste (optional)

Combine all the ingredients in a blender and blend until smooth.

LIME AND HONEY

2 tablespoons fresh lime juice

¼ cup water

¼ cup simple syrup (see page 237)

1 tablespoon honey

1 cup ice

Combine all the ingredients in a blender and blend until smooth.

STRAWBERRY AND LYCHEE

½ cup canned lychee fruit and syrup from the can

½ cup fresh strawberries, hulled

1 cup ice

Pinch of salt

Combine all the ingredients in a blender and blend until smooth.

NOTE: To cut the acidity of the fruit and add a little Thai kick, rim the glass with 2 parts salt and 1 part chile flakes.

WATERMELON AND THAI BASIL

1 cup seedless watermelon (cut into small chunks)

2 to 3 Thai basil leaves

1 cup ice

2 tablespoons honey, or to taste

Pinch of salt

Combine all the ingredients in a blender and blend until smooth.

THAI SODA

NAM SODA

MAKES 2 CUPS

I created these sodas to serve at parties as a way to introduce my friends to aromatic Thai flavors, especially the herbs, which are so versatile. Homemade soda is very refreshing and it can easily be upgraded with a shot of your favorite liquor (see my Thai Me Up! cocktail on page 180). In Thailand we toast with "Chon kaew," which means "Hit the glass!"

LEMONGRASS SYRUP

1 cup cane sugar or
   light brown sugar

1 cup water

4 stalks lemongrass,
   bruised

KRACHAI SYRUP

1 cup cane sugar or
   light brown sugar

1 cup water

1 cup krachai, very thinly
   sliced or shredded

GINGER OR GALANGAL SYRUP

1 cup cane sugar or
   light brown sugar

1 cup water

1 ($1\frac{1}{2}$-inch piece) ginger
   or galangal, cut into
   coins and bruised

KAFFIR LIME SYRUP

1 cup cane sugar or
   light brown sugar

1 cup water

12 kaffir lime leaves,
   torn 3 or 4 times to
   release their oils

THAI BASIL SYRUP

1 cup cane sugar or
   light brown sugar

1 cup water

$\frac{1}{2}$ cup whole Thai
   basil leaves

FOR THE SODA

Ice

Infused syrup

Soda water

TO MAKE THE SYRUP: In a small saucepan, combine the sugar and water. Place over medium heat and heat until the sugar is dissolved. Add the flavoring ingredient and mix well.

Remove from the heat, cover the pan, and let the syrup and flavoring steep for 1 hour. Strain and discard the solids. Store the syrup in an airtight container in the refrigerator for up to 2 weeks.

TO MAKE THE SODA: For one drink, fill a tall glass with ice. Add 3 tablespoons of the infused syrup of your choice, top with soda water, stir gently, and serve.

ซาเย็น

THAI ICED TEA

CHA YEN

MAKES 2 QUARTS

Brilliant orange and refreshingly sweet, Thai Iced Tea is the perfect thirst quencher in a hot and humid climate. Made from Thai tea powder (see page 243), water, and sugar, and sweetened with condensed milk, you can find it everywhere, like the lunch spot in Chiang Mai where I go for Chicken and Rice (page 67). It's delicious, easy to make, and the ingredients are all readily available pantry items so this might just become your new favorite drink.

1^1/$_3$ cups Thai tea powder

1^1/$_3$ cups sugar

Ice

Sweetened condensed milk, to taste

Bring 8 cups water to a boil in a large saucepan. Stir in the Thai tea powder and sugar.

Cover and remove from the heat to steep for 15 to 30 minutes, depending on desired strength. Strain the tea through a fine-mesh strainer and let cool.

Keep in an airtight container in the refrigerator for up to 2 weeks.

TO MAKE ONE DRINK: In a shaker, combine ice, 2 cups Thai iced tea, and 1 to 2 tablespoons condensed milk, or to taste, and shake well to blend. Serve over ice in a tall glass.

NOTE: For a less sweet, nondairy version, replace the condensed milk with fresh lime or lychee juice.

NGAM HOUSE COCKTAILS

EACH MAKES 1 DRINK

Sabai sabai ("Take it easy") is the mantra for Thai living. That's one reason Thailand is called the Land of Smiles. These cocktails embody the Thai way of life. Let them bring out the Thai in you. *Chon kaew!*

BELOW THE ROOT

2 tablespoons chopped lemongrass

2 or 3 thin slices ginger

½ ounce ginger syrup (page 175)

1 ounce lime juice

1²/3 ounces gin

Ice

Soda water

In a cocktail shaker, muddle the lemongrass with the ginger until well mashed. Pour in the ginger syrup, lime juice, and gin. Add ice and shake well. Strain into a tall glass filled with ice and top with a splash of soda.

EAST VILLAGER

1 lime

2 or 3 thin slices ginger

3 or 4 whole Thai basil leaves

½ ounce ginger syrup (page 175)

²/3 ounce triple sec

1 ounce tequila

Ice

Soda water

Cut the lime in half and cut 2 or 3 slices from one half. Juice the rest into a small bowl.

In a cocktail shaker, muddle all but one of the lime slices, ginger, and Thai basil leaves until well mashed. Pour in the ginger syrup, triple sec, tequila, and lime juice. Add ice and shake well. Strain into a glass filled with ice and top with a splash of soda and a slice of lime.

POMEGRANATE MARTINI

2 ounces pomegranate juice

1 ounce simple syrup

½ ounce lime juice

2½ ounces vodka

1 ounce triple sec

Ice

Lemon twist

Shake all the ingredients in a cocktail shaker over ice. Strain into a chilled martini glass and serve with a lemon twist.

THAI ICED TEA-TINI

2 ounces Thai Iced Tea (page 177)

1 ounce sweetened condensed milk

2 ounces vodka

Ice

Mint leaves

In a cocktail shaker, combine the Thai iced tea, condensed milk, vodka, and ice and shake well to chill. Strain into a martini glass, garnish with mint leaves, and serve.

THAI ME UP!

Chile Salt (recipe follows)

1 ounce Spicy and Aromatic Herb Syrup (recipe follows)

5 ounces cold Thai beer, preferably Singha

1 squeeze lime juice

Champagne

½ thinly sliced fresh long red Thai chile

kaffir lime leaves cut into thin chiffonade, or lemongrass cut into thin julienne

Pour the chile salt onto a saucer and rim a 10-ounce Champagne coupe with it.

Pour the herb syrup, beer, and lime juice into the glass and top with a splash of Champagne. Garnish with Thai chile, kaffir lime leaves, or lemongrass.

CHILE SALT

MAKES 2 TABLESPOONS

1 tablespoon salt

1 tablespoon red Thai chile powder

In a small bowl, mix the salt with Thai red chile powder until well mixed. Keep dry. This will keep the party going for a while. Repeat as needed.

SPICY AND AROMATIC HERB SYRUP

MAKES ABOUT 2 CUPS

2 cups sugar, preferably light brown sugar

2 cups water

1 stalk lemongrass, bruised

1 fresh red Thai chile, bruised

3 kaffir lime leaves, torn into 3 to 4 pieces

1 (1-inch) piece galangal, cut into 4 coins, each coin bruised

In a medium saucepan, dissolve the sugar in the water over medium-low heat. Add the lemongrass, chile, kaffir lime leaves, and galangal, cover, and remove from the heat. Steep the mixture for at least 2 hours or to taste—the longer it steeps, the spicier the syrup will be. Strain out the solids, transfer to a jar, cover, and keep refrigerated for up to 2 weeks.

NOTE: Combine 3 tablespoons of this spicy syrup with soda water over ice for a deliciously refreshing nonalcoholic drink (see page 175).

กระบอง

CHIANG MAI FRIES

KRAH BONG

SERVES 4 TO 6

I want to take you back with me to Warorot Market, the main market in the heart of Chiang Mai. When I was young, I used to love accompanying my mom there; she knew there was a stall where we could get *krah bong*, a traditional Chiang Mai snack of root vegetables fried in a red curry batter and served with sweet chile relish. Now the snack I loved as a kid in Chiang Mai is one of the best-selling items at my restaurant in New York City's East Village. It has been a road deliciously well traveled.

As a chef I have maintained the authenticity of *krabong* while adding a touch of Western cuisine with my red curry mayonnaise. They get along so well. Kabocha squash is becoming more and more common in farmers' markets and even grocery stores, but if you can't find it, feel free to use pumpkin or butternut squash.

2 quarts vegetable oil

1½ cups rice flour

1 (13.5-ounce) can coconut milk

2 tablespoons Red Curry Paste (page 229)

1 teaspoon salt, plus more to taste

½ cup dried unsweetened coconut flakes

½ medium kabocha squash, peeled and cut into ¼- to ½-inch-thick slices

1 yam, peeled and cut into ¼- to ½-inch-thick slices

Red Curry Mayonnaise (recipe follows)

Peanut Relish (recipe follows)

Heat the oil in a large high-sided skillet over medium-high heat until it reaches 375°F.

In a medium bowl, combine the rice flour, coconut milk, curry paste, 1 teaspoon salt, and the coconut and gently fold together into a thick batter.

Once the oil is ready, dip the squash and yam in the batter to lightly coat, let excess drip off, and then very carefully drop the slices one by one into the hot oil. Fry until golden brown and floating, 3 to 4 minutes.

Using a strainer or skimmer, remove the squash and yam to a paper towel–lined baking sheet and sprinkle with salt.

Transfer to a platter and serve with Red Curry Mayonnaise and Peanut Relish.

NOTE: In Thailand we make *krah bong* with many vegetables, including other members of the squash family and even green papaya.

RED CURRY MAYONNAISE

MAKES 1 CUP

1 cup mayonnaise
2 tablespoons Red Curry Paste (page 229)

In a small bowl, whisk the mayonnaise with
the red curry paste until fully incorporated.
Transfer to an airtight container and keep
refrigerated for up to 4 days.

PEANUT RELISH

MAKES ABOUT 1 CUP

1 cup white vinegar
½ cup sugar
1 fresh long red Thai chile
¼ cup finely chopped peanuts

In a small saucepan, combine the vinegar and sugar.
Place over medium heat and heat until the sugar is
dissolved. Remove from the heat and let cool. Transfer
to a blender, add the chile, and blend until well mixed.
Transfer to a bowl and stir in the peanuts.

หอยนางรมช๊อท

OYSTER SHOOTERS
WITH SPICY LIME AND CHILE SAUCE

HOI NANG ROM SHOT

MAKES 1

It wasn't until I moved to the United States that I fell in love with oysters, but I was never a fan of the traditional shallot and vinegar mignonette—their fresh, briny, and naturally sweet flavors seemed a natural match for *nam jim talay*. A round of these is a perfect *amuse-bouche* or hors d'oeuvre before a glamorous meal.

1 oyster, shucked and cleaned

1 (1½-inch) piece pomelo, from 1 peeled segment
    (or substitute ruby red grapefruit, mandarin,
    or blood orange)

½ teaspoon Spicy Lime and Chile Sauce (page 235)

Splash of Champagne or sparkling wine

½ teaspoon tobiko (flying fish roe)

1 to 2 kaffir lime leaves, cut into thin chiffonade

In a small shot glass or flute, layer the oyster, pomelo, Spicy Lime and Chile Sauce, champagne, and tobiko. Top with the kaffir lime leaves and serve.

ปอเปี๊ยะ

SPRING ROLLS

BAW BIA

MAKE 10 SPRING ROLLS

I love this snack. At Ngam we fry them to crispy perfection and serve them with my Orange-Ginger Dipping Sauce. It's a straightforward crowd-pleaser. Don't get frustrated when rolling your first batch—they don't have to be perfect, and you'll soon get the hang of it. Relax, have fun, and enjoy!

FOR THE FILLING

2 cups dried shiitake mushrooms

1 pound rice vermicelli noodles

½ cup vegetable oil

8 to 10 cloves garlic, minced

2 cups shredded carrots

3 to 4 sprigs cilantro, finely chopped

¼ cup mushroom sauce

1 tablespoon sugar

1 teaspoon freshly ground white pepper

FOR THE ROLLS

1 (12-ounce) package 8 × 8-inch spring roll wrappers

2 eggs, lightly beaten

FOR FRYING

2 quarts vegetable oil

Salt

Orange-Ginger Dipping Sauce (page 234)

MAKE THE FILLING: Soak the mushrooms in a bowl with warm water to cover until softened, 45 to 60 minutes. Drain and squeeze out excess water, then slice the caps into ¼-inch strips. Discard the mushroom stems and soaking liquid.

In a large bowl, submerge the noodles in room-temperature water to cover for at least 30 minutes or up to 1 hour, until softened, then cut them into 3- to 4-inch lengths.

Heat the oil in a wok or large sauté pan over medium heat until just sizzling. Add the garlic and sauté, stirring, until golden brown, about 30 seconds. Add the mushrooms, carrots, and cilantro and raise the heat to high. Stir-fry until the vegetables are just cooked, 2 to 3 minutes.

Add the noodles to the wok along with the mushroom sauce, sugar, and white pepper. Keep stirring until the noodles are coated with the sauce, about 3 minutes. Spread the filling onto a very lightly oiled baking sheet to cool the mixture down quickly. The filling can be made one day ahead and stored in a container in the refrigerator.

TO FILL THE SPRING ROLLS: Brush the edges of one wrapper with egg and spread 3 tablespoons of the cooled noodle mixture in a diagonal line down the center of the wrapper, leaving about 1 inch of space at both corners.

Fold in half diagonally and close the top triangle over the bottom, using your fingers to lightly press any remaining air out of the spring roll. Roll from the wide end to the point to form a tight cylinder and pinch the ends closed to seal a 1-inch border. Repeat with the remaining wrappers and noodle mixture.

TO FRY THE SPRING ROLLS: In a large saucepan, heat the oil to 375°F. Add 2 or 3 spring rolls to the oil at a time, being sure not to overcrowd the pan, and fry until golden brown, about 6 minutes, turning as necessary to fry them evenly. Using a slotted spoon or long-handled kitchen tongs, transfer to a cooling rack set on a paper towel–lined baking sheet to drain and season with salt. Cut each spring roll into 2 to 4 pieces and serve hot with Orange-Ginger Dipping Sauce.

ทอดมันข้าวโพดกับอาจาด

SWEET CORN FRITTERS WITH CUCUMBER RELISH

TOD MUN KHAO POTE GAP AJARD

MAKES ABOUT 20 FRITTERS

This recipe was inspired by *tod mun*, my favorite snack when I was a little girl. After moving to New York City, it was deliciously comforting to re-create one of my most beloved flavors from childhood with my new love for sweet corn from the fantastic local farms that supply Ngam. I feel confident that you will make it again and again and it will become a favorite summer recipe.

6 to 8 cups vegetable oil

2 cups fresh corn kernels (from 2 to 3 ears corn), blanched

1 tablespoon Red Curry Paste (page 229)

2 large eggs, lightly beaten

¼ cup coconut milk

½ cup rice flour or all-purpose flour

½ cup dried unsweetened shredded coconut

½ teaspoon salt, plus more to taste

2 teaspoons sugar

2 to 3 kaffir lime leaves, cut into thin chiffonade

Cucumber Relish (page 226)

In a large saucepan, heat the oil to 375°F.

In a large bowl, combine the corn, curry paste, eggs, coconut milk, rice flour, coconut, ½ teaspoon salt, the sugar, and kaffir lime leaves until well blended into a thick batter, almost a paste.

Carefully drop rounded tablespoons of the batter into the oil, a few at a time, and fry until golden brown, 3 to 4 minutes per batch. Using a slotted spoon, transfer the fritters to a paper towel–lined baking sheet to drain and season with salt. Serve hot with Cucumber Relish.

ต้มโคล้ง

THE 15-MINUTE SOUP
THAT CHANGED MY LIFE

TOM KHLONG

SERVES 4

Not in a million years would I ever have thought I would be a challenger on a show like *Iron Chef America*, going up against Iron Chef Bobby Flay, himself. Since the "secret ingredient" for my challenge was tamarind, I immediately thought of *tom khlong*—a delicious soup full of pungent tamarind flavor. And the best thing about it is that it's fast! Though traditionally served with crispy fish, I chose to pair it with crispy soft-shell crab for its great texture and flavor and to elevate the dish a bit for the competition. This sour-sweet-spicy soup put me in an early lead and made the Iron Chef sweat—in more ways than one!

1 quart vegetable oil

1½ cups rice flour

Salt and freshly ground black pepper

1 cup soda water

4 small soft-shell crabs, cleaned

4 stalks lemongrass

½ cup sliced galangal

6 kaffir lime leaves, torn into quarters

4 dried red Thai chiles, toasted in a dry skillet and broken in half

2 shallots, cut into quarters and bruised

¼ cup halved cherry tomatoes

6 cups Thai Seafood Stock (page 237)

¼ cup tamarind concentrate

3 tablespoons fish sauce

2 tablespoons palm sugar

¼ cup whole Thai basil leaves

Coarsely chopped cilantro and culantro

Heat the oil in a wok or medium saucepan to 375°F.

In a medium bowl, season 1 cup rice flour with salt and pepper. Carefully pour in the soda water, stirring to form a batter.

Dust the crabs on both sides with the remaining ½ cup rice flour and shake off excess flour.

Dip each crab in the batter and fry until golden brown on both sides, about 3 minutes per side. Using a slotted spoon, carefully remove the crabs to a baking sheet lined with paper towels to drain. Season with salt.

Combine the lemongrass stalks, galangal, kaffir lime leaves, chiles, shallots, and tomatoes in a medium saucepan. Place over high heat and heat until lightly blackened and fragrant, 3 to 5 minutes. Add the stock to the mixture and bring to a boil. Lower the heat and season with tamarind concentrate, fish sauce, and sugar. Off the heat, stir in the Thai basil.

Place 1 crispy crab in each of four soup bowls and pour the hot soup over them. Garnish with a sprinkle of cilantro and culantro and serve.

ยำจิ้นไก่

RUSTIC CHICKEN SOUP

YUM JIN GAI

SERVES 4 TO 6

There's an almost romantic quality to this soup. I have been in love with its flavor since one of my grade school classmates brought it to a potluck party. It also happens to be the soup that brought my favorite actor to my kitchen. One fall afternoon as I was preparing for our dinner service at Ngam, a familiar face walked in the door. OMG, I thought in my head. This man has been my favorite actor since I was in eighth grade! But surely I can't tell him that . . . I am a professional cook. I am here to serve, not to make friends. He took two quarts of this soup to go, and came back the next day for more. And again the next day. And the next. Pure magic!

2 quarts water

4 stalks lemongrass, cut into 2-inch pieces and bruised

½ cup sliced galangal (¼- to ½-inch coins)

4 pieces fresh turmeric (about the size of your little finger), bruised

3 pounds bone-in chicken breasts and thighs

¼ cup thinly sliced shallot

2 tablespoons thinly sliced scallion

¼ cup coarsely chopped cilantro

½ cup coarsely chopped mint

½ cup coarsely chopped bamboo mint

½ cup coarsely chopped culantro

2 teaspoons *Laab* Chile (page 83), or to taste

2 tablespoons fish sauce, or to taste

In a large saucepan, combine the water, lemongrass, galangal, and turmeric. Place over high heat and bring to a boil. Add the chicken, return to a boil, then lower the heat to maintain a simmer and cook until the chicken is cooked through, 10 to 15 minutes.

Reduce the heat to low and remove the chicken from the pan to a plate to cool, then finely shred it. Remove the lemongrass, galangal, and turmeric from the pot and discard them. Return the shredded chicken to the pot. Bring the mixture back to a boil, then add the shallot, scallion, cilantro, mint, the culantro, the *Laab* Chile, and fish sauce—the broth will be spicy, slightly salty, and very aromatic from the herbs. Spoon into bowls and serve.

NOTE: In my hometown, we consider this dish a salad, which is why it's called *yum jin gai* (which literally translates to "salad of chicken meat"). I love the flavor so much that whenever I make it I want more and more of the broth, so I went ahead and turned it into a comforting and hearty soup.

ซุปข้าวโพด

THAI CORN CHOWDER

SOUP KHAO POTE

SERVES 4 TO 6

I love the sunny flavor of fresh sweet corn, which also grows in Thailand, and came up with this recipe the first summer Ngam was open. I wanted to showcase the beautiful local corn with traditional ingredients like coconut milk and Thai herbs. It's super flavorful, super healthful, and equally delicious served hot or chilled.

2 tablespoons coconut cream or coconut oil

3 cloves garlic, roughly chopped

2 small shallots, roughly chopped

Kernels from 10 ears sweet corn

5 kaffir lime leaves

2/3 cup whole Thai basil leaves

8 to 10 stalks lemongrass (bottom 2 to 3 inches only) sliced

1 to 2 dried red Thai chiles

6 (13.5-ounce) cans coconut milk

1/3 cup palm sugar

2 teaspoons salt

Coconut water, if serving cold

In a medium saucepan, heat the coconut cream over medium heat until just bubbling. Add the garlic and shallots and cook, stirring, until fragrant, about 3 minutes. Add the corn, kaffir lime leaves, Thai basil, lemongrass, and chiles and cook for another 5 minutes to sweat the ingredients. Add the coconut milk and bring to a boil, then add the sugar and salt, lower the heat, and simmer for about 10 minutes, until the flavors are well incorporated and the corn is tender.

To serve hot, remove from heat and allow cool for a few minutes, then working in batches, pour the mixture into a blender and blend until smooth. Return the soup to the saucepan and reheat. Serve hot.

To serve cold, gradually thin the blended chowder with coconut water to your liking (the chowder will thicken as it cools), cover, and chill in the refrigerator.

ยำเคลกับเห็ด

SPICY KALE AND MUSHROOM SALAD

YUM KALE KUB HET

SERVES 4

I am so grateful that my restaurant is near the Union Square Greenmarket, the largest farmers' market in New York City. The bounty of farm-fresh vegetables is heaven! The first time I tasted local kale, my mind went straight to *yum ka na*, a traditional Thai salad made with *pak ka na*, or Chinese broccoli. In this version, I have added meaty and delicious mushrooms, which pair so well with the spicy dressing along with the crunchy kale. This dish is my go-to superfood.

4 cups kale leaves or baby kale, cut into
 ¼-inch-thick strips

1 king oyster mushroom, sliced into
 ½-inch-thick coins (about 2 cups)

1 shallot, thinly sliced

¼ cup Spicy Lime and Chile Sauce (page 235)

In a large bowl, combine the kale, mushroom, and shallot and toss with the sauce to coat.

ส้าปลาแซลมอน

CHIANG MAI–INSPIRED SALMON TIRATIDO

SAA SALMON

SERVES 2

Saa is the way northern Thais cook their meat, slicing it instead of grinding it like with *laab*. I was fortunate to learn more about this dish in the kitchen of Le Grand Lanna at the Mandarin Oriental Dhara Dhevi Chiang Mai; I first tried it at a family meal shared with the kitchen staff when I was an intern there. It was so delicious that it inspired me to include a twist on the original on my menu at Ngam in New York City, where we pair the salmon with avocado and grapefruit and season it with authentic northern Thai flavors.

1 grapefruit

6 ounces raw salmon fillet, thinly sliced

5 mint leaves, cut into thin chiffonade

1 stalk lemongrass, thinly sliced

2 kaffir lime leaves, cut into thin chiffonade

1 shallot, thinly sliced

½ avocado, peeled and cut into ¼-inch slices

1 teaspoon Toasted Rice Powder (page 227)

1 teaspoon *Laab* Chile (page 83), or to taste

2 tablespoons lime juice

1 tablespoon fish sauce

Working over a bowl to catch the juice, supreme the grapefruit: Using a sharp paring knife, separate and remove the membrane from each segment.

Add the segments and the remaining ingredients to the bowl, gently mix and serve.

For a more elegant presentation, you can also mix the juices, herbs, shallot, chiles, and fish sauce in a mixing bowl. Divide the salmon, grapefruit, and avocado slices among small plates, alternating layers, and top with the juice mixture.

THAI GARDEN SALAD
WITH *MIANG* DRESSING

YUM MIANG KHAM

SERVES 4

This salad is inspired by my grandmother's favorite snack, Betel Bites (page 23). Traditionally it's made with betel leaves coated with ginger, chiles, peanuts, toasted coconut, and a sticky caramel jam made from palm sugar, tamarind, and fish sauce. I don't let the scarcity of betel leaves in New York stop me from enjoying the beauty of this dish; instead, I replace the betel leaves with the freshest mesclun or microgreens available at the nearby Union Square Greenmarket, which I toss in the traditional tangy *mieng* dressing.

FOR THE *MIANG* DRESSING

½ cup palm sugar

2 tablespoons mushroom sauce

4 tablespoons tamarind concentrate

2 tablespoons finely diced ginger

1 to 3 fresh red Thai chiles

½ cup grapeseed oil

FOR THE SALAD

5 ounces mesclun greens (about 6 to 8 cups)

1 cup dried unsweetened shredded coconut

¼ cup ginger cut into thin chiffonade

½ lime, sliced and each slice quartered, or diced

Organic edible flowers, such as rose petals, nasturtiums, or pansies (see Note), some reserved for garnish

1 cup toasted and coarsely chopped peanuts

MAKE THE *MIANG* DRESSING: In a small saucepan, combine the sugar, mushroom sauce, and tamarind concentrate. Place over medium heat and stir until the sugar is dissolved and the ingredients are well combined. Remove from the heat and let cool.

Pour the cooled sugar mixture into a blender, add the ginger and chiles, and blend until smooth. Gradually add the oil through the hole in the top 2 tablespoons at a time to emulsify the dressing.

MAKE THE SALAD: In a large bowl, gently toss the greens, coconut, ginger, lime, flowers (save those reserved for garnish), and peanuts with the dressing until just coated. Top the salad or each individual serving with the reserved blossoms.

NOTE: Edible flowers are a delicacy; added to salads and other fresh dishes, their soft petals and softer flavors add bright color, rustic texture, and subtle perfume. Look closely when you shop for fresh greens at the farmers' market, especially in late spring and high summer; most local farms will also offer beautiful assortments of blossoms that are as safe to eat as any salad greens.

ผัดไทย

OLD-SCHOOL PAD THAI WITH SHRIMP

PAD THAI

SERVES 4

Pad thai may be the one Thai dish everyone knows—or thinks they know. A tangy-sweet stir-fry of rice noodles, egg, often chicken or shrimp, and topped with fresh bean sprouts, chopped peanuts, and lime, it's the national dish of Thailand and a perpetual favorite on takeout menus worldwide. Made properly, it can be as sublimely complex and flavorful as any Thai dish. I first made this version for my boss, Chef Greg Brainin, and later for Chef Jean-Georges, himself, while still a prep cook at Spice Market. Between bites, Chef Jean-Georges looked at me with new respect and said, "Wow, this tastes just like the *pad thai* I've had in Thailand. Who taught you how to cook?" I've never been more thankful for all the time spent by Grandma Prapit's side! At Ngam, we also serve *pad thai* with thinly sliced chicken, pork, or even roasted duck in place of the shrimp.

FOR THE SAUCE

½ cup tamarind concentrate

½ cup palm sugar

½ cup fish sauce

FOR THE *PAD THAI*

8 ounces rice stick noodles

2 tablespoons vegetable oil

6 cloves garlic, finely chopped

2 small shallots, finely chopped

1 tablespoon pickled turnip minced

4 jumbo shrimp, peeled and deveined

2 eggs, preferably farm-fresh

½ cup diced extra-firm tofu

½ cup chives cut into 1-inch lengths

½ cup bean sprouts

2 tablespoons crushed peanuts

Red Thai chile powder

Lime wedges

TO MAKE THE SAUCE: Combine the tamarind concentrate, sugar, and fish sauce in a small saucepan. Place over medium-high heat and bring to a boil, then reduce the heat to low and cook for about 10 minutes, until the sauce thickens enough to coat the back of a spoon. Remove from the heat and set aside.

TO MAKE THE *PAD THAI*: Place the rice stick noodles in a shallow dish and add room-temperature water (don't use hot or warm water—this will turn the noodles mushy) to cover. Leave to soak until just al dente, up to 45 minutes depending on the noodles. Keep the hydrated noodles in the water until ready to use.

Heat the oil in a cast-iron skillet or wok over high heat. Add the garlic, shallots, and pickled turnip and cook, stirring, until the garlic is fragrant, about 1 minute, watching carefully so it does not brown.

Add the shrimp and cook, stirring, for 1 to 2 minutes, just until pink. Remove the cooked shrimp to a bowl and set aside.

Increase the heat to high and crack the eggs over the garlic and shallots. Using a spatula or wooden spoon, break the yolks and stir gently, but do not scramble. Cook for another 1 to 2 minutes, until fully cooked. Add the drained noodles and the sauce and stir until the noodles have softened and are coated with the sauce and egg mixture. Add the cooked shrimp and the tofu and mix well. Stir in the chives, bean sprouts, and peanuts and remove from the heat.

Serve on a platter garnished with a sprinkling of chile powder and lime wedges.

NOTE: As with many of the stir-fries in this book, the key to a good pad Thai is high heat, which is why I recommend a large cast-iron skillet over a wok for home use. In Thailand, true old-school *pad thai* is traditionally cooked on a flat-topped iron pan on a charcoal stove. Trust me, using the right heat and pan will help ensure the best finished texture for the noodles and promotes the caramelization of the sauce, glazing the noodles for the truest flavor. If you are using a very wide pan, make sure to keep an eye on everything, as it will cook fast over high heat.

ผัดไทยมะละกอ ผัดไทยซูกินี่กุ้งสด

PAPAYA OR ZUCCHINI *PAD THAI* WITH SHRIMP

PAD THAI MALAKO, PAD THAI ZUCCHINI GOONG SOT

SERVES 2 TO 4

I probably should thank Chef Mario Batali for inspiring this low-carb version of the classic Thai noodle dish: Watching him make zucchini pasta gave me the idea, and it's now one of the most popular menu items at Ngam. The shredded zucchini and papaya both stay toothsome and bring a fresh brightness to the dish that complements the sweet and tangy *pad thai* flavors. I like to give the shrimp a good sear to go atop this dish, so I use jumbo shrimp or prawns and a good hot pan. It's essential to air-dry the shredded papaya or zucchini overnight in the refrigerator to achieve the desired texture, so plan accordingly.

FOR THE SAUCE

¼ cup tamarind concentrate

¼ cup palm sugar

¼ cup fish sauce

FOR THE *PAD THAI*

2 tablespoons vegetable oil, plus more for cooking the shrimp

4 jumbo shrimp or prawns, peeled and deveined

2 teaspoons minced garlic

2 teaspoons finely chopped shallot

1 egg

1 large green papaya or 2 medium zucchinis, julienned (about 3 cups), placed on a baking sheet, and air-dried overnight in the refrigerator

½ cup extra-firm tofu cut into ½-inch cubes

1 tablespoon diced pickled turnip

2 to 3 Chinese chives, cut into 1-inch pieces (about ½ cup)

1 cup bean sprouts

2 tablespoons crushed peanuts

Red Thai chile powder

Lime wedges

TO MAKE THE SAUCE: Combine the sauce ingredients in a bowl and stir until well incorporated. Set aside.

TO MAKE THE *PAD THAI*: Coat the surface of a heavy skillet with vegetable oil. Place over high heat, add the shrimp, and cook until just pink and no longer translucent, turning once, about 4 minutes. Brush lightly with the sauce, then remove from the heat and set aside.

In a wok or large skillet, heat the 2 tablespoons oil over medium heat. Add the garlic and shallot and cook until fragrant, about 1 minute, taking care not to let it brown. Increase the heat to high and crack the egg over the pan. Break the yolk and stir gently, but do not scramble. Cook for 1 to 2 minutes, until the egg is fully cooked. Add the shredded papaya or zucchini and the rest of the sauce and cook, stirring, until the vegetables are softened, about 1 minute. Add the cooked shrimp, the tofu, and pickled turnip and toss to mix well. Stir in the chives, bean sprouts, and peanuts. Spoon into dishes and sprinkle each with a little chile powder and serve with a lime wedge.

เส้นหมึกดำผัดพริกไทยดำกับปลาหมึกกรอบ

THE DARK KNIGHT

SEN MUEK DAM PAD PRIK THAI DAM KUB PLA MUEK KROB

SERVES 4

The components of this dish are inspired by different times and places in my life. I learned how to make the black pepper sauce while interning at the Mandarin Oriental Dhara Dhevi. Fried calamari was one of the best-selling items when I was a line cook at Perry Street; I've made my own version using a black pepper batter. Ever since its debut on our menu, this peppery, sweet, and salty dish has been one of the restaurant's star dishes. We make our own noodles at Ngam, but you can find squid-ink pasta in Italian markets, specialty pasta shops, or online.

FOR THE CALAMARI

- 2 quarts vegetable oil
- 1 cup rice flour or all-purpose flour
- 1 teaspoon freshly ground black pepper, plus more to taste
- 1 teaspoon salt, plus more to taste
- 1 cup soda water
- 3 ounces calamari, sliced into ½-inch rings

FOR THE NOODLES

- 2 tablespoons vegetable oil
- 1 tablespoon finely chopped garlic
- 2 cups cooked squid-ink noodles
- 1 fresh long red Thai chile, sliced ½ inch thick
- 1 cup quartered Brussels sprouts
- 4 tablespoons oyster sauce
- 1½ tablespoons mushroom sauce
- 2 tablespoons white wine
- 2 teaspoons freshly ground black pepper
- 1 small sprig cilantro, chopped
- 1 lime, cut into wedges

TO MAKE THE CALAMARI: In a medium saucepan, heat the oil over medium-high heat to 375°F.

In a medium bowl, combine ½ cup of the flour, the black pepper, and salt. Add the soda water and blend until well mixed. In a separate bowl, dust the calamari rings with the remaining flour and toss to coat. Shake off the excess and dip in the batter to coat.

A few at a time, carefully add the battered rings to the oil. Fry the calamari until golden brown and crispy, 3 to 4 minutes. Don't overcrowd the pan, and work in batches if necessary. Using a slotted spoon, transfer the fried calamari rings to a paper towel–lined baking sheet and season with salt and pepper.

TO MAKE THE NOODLES: Heat the oil in a wok or sauté pan over medium-high heat. Add the garlic and sauté, stirring, until fragrant, about 2 minutes, being careful not to let it burn. Add the noodles, chile, and Brussels sprouts, then add the oyster sauce, mushroom sauce, wine, and black pepper and cook, stirring, for 2 to 3 minutes, until well incorporated and the Brussels sprouts are cooked.

Mound the stir-fried noodles and vegetables onto a plate and top with a handful of hot calamari rings. Sprinkle with chopped cilantro and serve with lime wedges.

ไก่ย่าง

GRILLED CHICKEN

GAI YANG

It's a privilege to work with Cascun Farm in upstate New York to bring the highest quality chicken to the table at my restaurant. Even if you can't get farm-fresh chicken, buy the best chicken you can find. This dish will really show it off. But don't get fancy or bring out your finest silver, because the best way to enjoy this chicken is with your hands! Alongside Green Papaya Salad (page 139) and sticky rice (page 82), this is a perfect summer meal. At Ngam we serve this with our homemade Spicy Tamarind Sauce. I speak for many of our guests in saying that it's addictive!

1 farm-raised chicken (about 3 pounds), butterflied
2 cups Ngam's House Marinade (page 227)
Chopped cilantro
Spicy Tamarind Dipping Sauce (page 235)

In a large bowl, marinate the chicken in the marinade for at least 2 hours or overnight.

Heat a charcoal grill to medium heat. Place the chicken on the grill with skin side down. Grill for about 15 minutes, brushing with the marinade. Turn and repeat on the other side, cooking until the chicken is cooked through. Transfer to a platter and serve garnished with chopped cilantro and the sauce alongside.

เสือดีใจ

HAPPY TIGER

SUA DEE JAI

SERVES 4

The origin of this dish is Isan, from northeastern Thailand. Thai legend has it that tigers cry over the fact that men take all the cows, a meat that tigers love. My version of this dish fits more into my belief system—why be sad? Let's be happy. To perk up the tigers—and with the help of my new friends at Brooklyn Roasting Company—I give the steak a rich, delicious crust of freshly ground coffee and salt, then serve it with Issan-Style Dipping Sauce (page 234) and Cucumber Relish (page 226).

1 cup Ngam's House Marinade (page 227)

1 pound steak of your choice (any cut works, from aged strip to skirt or hangar steak)

½ cup freshly ground coffee of your choice (slightly coarsely ground)

Salt

Issan-Style Dipping Sauce

Cucumber Relish

Rub the marinade over the meat in a medium bowl and place in the refrigerator to marinate for at least 30 minutes or up to overnight. Remove the meat from the refrigerator and pat dry.

Press the ground coffee evenly all over both sides of the steak and season with salt (the marinade will have flavored the meat already, but you want to season the crust as well).

The coffee-and-salt crust works for many preparations, including the traditional grilling over coals (medium heat, 4 minutes per side for medium-rare), searing in a cast-iron skillet, or even broiling, depending on your chosen steak.

Let the steaks rest for about 10 minutes. Thinly slice and serve with the cucumber, long beans, cabbage, and tomatoes, and Issan-Style Dipping Sauce on the side.

ปลานึ่งขิงกับน้ำจิ้มทะเล

SPICY STEAMED BASS WITH GINGER

PLA NUENG KHING GUB NAM JIM TALAY

SERVES 1 OR 2

The more I cook, the more I learn the truth behind the saying "You are what you eat." I feel it's my responsibility to come up with recipes that are not only flavorful but also good for you. And now that I am sharing my recipes with you, I want to make sure they're also easy to make at home. This dish is all of that: sweet and sour with the aroma of ginger, containing almost no fat, and only one pan to clean! It's easy to double or even triple the recipe to serve guests—just make sure you don't crowd the pan.

½ cup Spicy Lime and Chile Sauce (page 235)

¼ cup Thai Seafood Stock (page 237), Thai Chicken Stock (page 236), or water

1 (8-ounce) bass fillet

2 tablespoons julienned ginger

1 tablespoon thinly sliced shallot

1 tablespoon coarsely chopped toasted cashews

Hot steamed jasmine or brown rice

Heat a heavy skillet with a lid over medium-high heat. Add ¼ cup of the Spicy Lime and Chile Sauce and the stock to the center of the skillet and immediately top with the bass fillet and 1 tablespoon of the ginger and half of the shallot. Cover and cook for 4 to 5 minutes, until the fish is opaque and just cooked through. Be careful lifting the lid, as there will be a lot of (very fragrant) steam coming out. Place on a platter.

In small bowl, mix the remaining ¼ cup Spicy Lime and Chile Sauce with the remaining 1 tablespoon ginger, remaining shallot, and cashews. Top the fish with the herb salad and serve with steamed jasmine or brown rice.

ไส้อั่วเบอร์เกอร์

MY THAI BURGER

SAI OOA BURGER

SERVES 6

This burger was inspired by a traditional sausage dish from Chiang Mai (page 64). Topped with homemade cilantro-lime mayonnaise and pickled green papaya, it's a fresh, Thai take on the American classic. I used to make it for friends when I first moved to Brooklyn and it has since become one of the most popular menu items at Ngam, getting us the attention of the *Wall Street Journal*, the *Village Voice*, *Zagat*, and more. Serve with Chiang Mai Fries (page 182).

5 dried long red Thai chiles, seeded

1 tablespoon black soy sauce

2 tablespoons Thai fish sauce

1½ teaspoons salt

10 kaffir lime leaves, finely chopped (about 1 tablespoon)

¼ cup sliced lemongrass

¼ cup garlic, roughly chopped

¼ cup roughly chopped shallot

2 teaspoons peeled and chopped fresh turmeric

3 pounds ground beef

Vegetable oil or cooking spray

6 hamburger buns

Cilantro-Lime Mayonnaise (recipe follows)

6 slices tomato

Pickled Green Papaya Slaw (recipe follows)

Place the dried chiles in a small bowl and add warm water to cover. Leave to soften for about 15 minutes. Wearing kitchen gloves (do not use bare hands when working with chiles), remove the chiles from the water and squeeze out excess water.

In the bowl of a food processor, combine the hydrated chiles, black soy sauce, fish sauce, salt, kaffir lime leaves, lemongrass, garlic, shallot, and turmeric. Pulse until it forms a paste, about 3 minutes. Transfer to a large bowl, add the beef, and knead gently together just until well incorporated, but be careful not to overwork the meat. Divide the mixture into 6 balls and flatten into patties with the heel of your hand. Place on a plate, cover with plastic, and refrigerate the patties for at least 2 hours, or preferably overnight, to fully absorb the seasoning.

Remove the patties from the refrigerator and bring to room temperature to ensure even cooking. Preheat a grill or a cast-iron skillet over medium-high heat and lightly coat the cooking surface with oil. Grill or sear the burgers to your desired doneness, 3 to 4 minutes per side. Partly covering the grill or skillet will help the meat stay moist.

While the burgers rest, toast the buns on the hot grill until golden, about 1 minute.

Place the burgers on the toasted bottom bun and top with the mayonnaise, sliced tomato, and papaya slaw.

CILANTRO-LIME MAYONNAISE

MAKES ABOUT 1 CUP

2 egg yolks

1 cup canola oil

1 teaspoon salt

1 tablespoon lime juice

2 tablespoons minced cilantro

Grated zest of 1 lime

1 teaspoon freshly ground black pepper

Place the yolks in the bowl of an electric stand mixer. Beat the eggs on the highest setting until they turn a light yellow color, about 2 minutes.

While the mixer is running, slowly add the oil, about ½ teaspoon at a time. Be careful not add too much oil too quickly or the oil and egg will separate. Once the mayonnaise looks fluffy and glossy, remove from the mixer and fold in the remaining ingredients.

NOTE: You can also use 1 cup jarred mayonnaise in place of the egg yolks and oil and simply stir in the remaining ingredients.

PICKLED GREEN PAPAYA SLAW

MAKES ABOUT 2 CUPS

½ cup tamarind concentrate

½ cup fish sauce

½ cup palm sugar

1½ cups shredded green papaya

Prepare an ice water bath.

In a medium saucepan, combine the tamarind concentrate, fish sauce, and sugar. Place over medium-high heat and stir until the sugar is completely dissolved. Transfer to a medium bowl and set in the ice water bath to cool to room temperature, about 5 minutes. Add the shredded papaya and stir to combine. Set aside to pickle for about 1 hour.

ข้าวผัดแกงเขียวหวาน

GREEN CURRY FRIED RICE

KHAO PAD GAENG KHIAW WAN

SERVES 4

I love the flavor of green curry—sweet, coconut-y, with the aromatic touch of Thai basil and just a little heat. I am also a simple girl who loves fried rice! So I merged the two to make it into a bowl of lovely, hearty flavor. This makes a great side dish or a whole meal in itself.

½ cup coconut milk

¼ cup Green Curry Paste (page 229)

1 cup protein of your choice, such as chicken, pork or beef tenderloin, or tofu cut into bite-size pieces or whole peeled and deveined medium shrimp

½ cup diced Japanese or Thai eggplant

4 cups steamed and cooled jasmine or brown rice (leftover rice works best)

½ cup whole Thai basil leaves

¼ cup sliced fresh long red Thai chiles

1 tablespoon fish sauce (or mushroom sauce for vegetarians), or to taste

1 tablespoon palm sugar, or to taste

2 tablespoons toasted unsweetened coconut flakes (optional)

Heat a wok or wide sauté pan over medium-high heat. Add the coconut cream and green curry paste and cook, stirring, until the color turns a deeper green and the aroma intensifies, 2 to 3 minutes. Add the protein and stir until it's cooked (about 5 minutes for chicken, pork, and beef; about 3 minutes for shrimp; about 2 minutes for tofu). Add the eggplant, then the rice, and continue to cook, stirring, until well mixed. Lower the heat to medium, add the Thai basil and chiles, and cook, stirring, for 2 minutes. Remove from the heat and season with the fish sauce and sugar.

Transfer to a bowl and serve, sprinkled with the toasted coconut flakes, if using.

ข้าวผัดเคล

KALE FRIED RICE

KHAO PAD KALE

SERVES 4

This recipe is Thai with a twist. It's inspired by *khao pad kana*, or fried rice with Chinese broccoli. As a proud New Yorker now, I love to introduce local flavors and ingredients into traditional Thai dishes, and here kale from the Union Square Greenmarket steps in. We live in a global world but can eat like locals. Support local farms!

2 tablespoons vegetable oil

1 tablespoon chopped garlic

3 eggs

½ cup cup halved cherry tomatoes

¼ cup chopped onion

1 cup protein of your choice, such as chicken, pork or beef tenderloin, or tofu cut into bite-size pieces or whole peeled and deveined medium shrimp

4 cups steamed and cooled jasmine or brown rice (leftover rice is great!)

1 cup chopped kale leaves

2 tablespoons mushroom sauce or soy sauce, to taste

2 teaspoons sugar, to taste

Freshly ground white or black pepper

Garnishes: cilantro sprigs, scallions, sliced cucumber, lime wedges, Fish Sauce with Chiles (page 226), extra-crispy fried egg (optional)

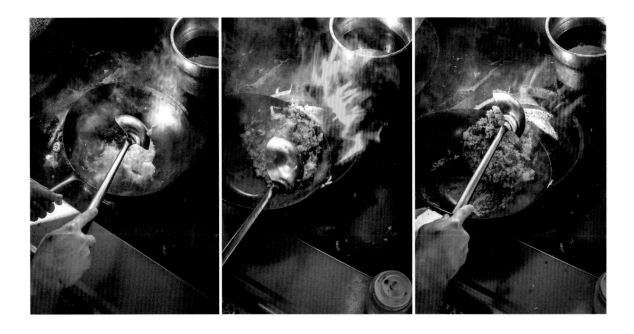

Heat the oil in a wok or wide sauté pan over medium-high heat. Add the garlic and cook, stirring, until fragrant, being careful not to let it burn, about 2 minutes.

Crack the eggs into the wok and break the yolks in the pan with a wooden spatula. Add the tomatoes, onion, and protein of your choice. Cook, stirring, until cooked through, about 3 minutes. Add the rice and kale and cook until the kale just wilts, about 3 minutes. Season with mushroom sauce, sugar, and white pepper to taste and toss to coat.

Serve with cilantro sprigs, scallions, sliced cucumber, lime wedges, and a side of Fish Sauce with Chiles with or without a fried egg.

NOTE: *Khao pad* is a versatile basic preparation that can be varied to whatever ingredients you have on hand or like to use. It's so simple I was tossing it together for friends at ten years old using rice from dinner the night before, fresh eggs, Maggi sauce (a common Thai pantry staple), a little sugar, and sliced cucumbers for crunch. Follow the basic proportions of this recipe using leftovers or pantry staples and you can have *khao pad* anytime. For an all-American version of the Thai classic, try it with leftover roast turkey, cooked squash or sweet potatoes, green vegetables, and gravy—Thanksgiving Fried Rice!

ฟักทองผัดไข่ใส่โหระพา

PUMPKIN AND THAI BASIL

FAK TONG PAD KHAI SAI HORAPA

SERVES 2 TO 4

This is a wonderful traditional dish for the fall, when squash are at their peak. The combination of sweet, earthy pumpkin and spicy Thai basil is a match made in heaven. You can try kabocha, butternut, delicata, or any favorite winter squash in place of the pumpkin—I love to ask the farmers at the Union Square Greenmarket if they have new varieties to try.

2 cups peeled and cubed pumpkin or winter squash
   (2-inch cubes)

2 tablespoons vegetable oil

2 cloves garlic, chopped

2 eggs

1 cup whole Thai basil leaves

1 fresh red Thai long chile, thinly sliced into rounds

2 tablespoons oyster sauce

1 teaspoon brown sugar (optional)

Hot steamed jasmine or brown rice

Bring a large pot of water to a boil. Add the pumpkin and blanch for 5 minutes, until just tender. Drain and rinse under cold water to stop the cooking. Set aside.

Heat the oil in a wok or a sauté pan over medium-high heat. Add the garlic and sauté, stirring, until golden and aromatic, about 2 minutes. Add the eggs and stir to break the yolks, but do not scramble. Cook for 1 to 2 minutes, until the eggs are still soft but cooked through. Add the blanched pumpkin, the Thai basil, chile, oyster sauce, and brown sugar, if using, and cook for another 3 to 5 minutes. Remove from the heat and serve with steamed jasmine or brown rice.

พายฟักทอง

THAI RED CURRY PUMPKIN PIE

PIE FAK TONG

MAKES 1 (9½-INCH) PIE

I know you are probably wondering, *What is she thinking, putting an American classic in a Thai cookbook?!* Well, here's why I'm including this recipe: I love, love, *LOVE* pumpkin pie! Here red curry and Thai basil put a fragrant, spicy spin on classic pumpkin pie flavors. This dessert is a tribute to the country that has given me the opportunity to dream big and share my love for Thai food. I believe this could become a new Thai-American classic.

FOR THE CRUST

¾ cup all-purpose flour

4 tablespoons unsalted butter, at room temperature

1 to 2 tablespoons milk

FOR THE FILLING

2 cups peeled and cubed kabocha squash
   or pumpkin (2-inch cubes)

2 large eggs

½ cup palm sugar

2 tablespoons granulated sugar

2 tablespoons Red Curry Paste (page 229)

1²/₃ cups coconut milk

Salt

FOR THE RED CURRY CREAM

½ cup very cold heavy cream

1 teaspoon sugar

1 tablespoon Red Curry Paste (page 229)

FOR THE CANDIED THAI BASIL

10 whole Thai basil leaves

1 egg white, lightly whisked

½ cup sugar

TO MAKE THE CRUST: In a large bowl, roll pinches of the flour and butter lightly between your fingertips until you have a loose, sandy texture with pea-size lumps. Add 1 tablespoon milk and stir gently to form a loose ball, adding up to another tablespoon of milk if needed.

Turn the ball onto a lightly floured work surface and gently form it into a round. Wrap the dough tightly in plastic wrap and chill in the refrigerator for at least 30 minutes or up to 1 hour.

Preheat the oven to 425°F.

TO MAKE THE FILLING: Set a steamer insert with the pumpkin in a medium saucepan and add a couple inches of water to the pot, just enough to steam the pumpkin but not come directly into contact with it. Bring to a simmer and steam for about 10 minutes, until just cooked through. Remove from the heat and set aside to cool.

In a blender, combine the cooled pumpkin, the eggs, palm sugar, granulated sugar, curry paste, coconut milk, and a pinch of salt and blend until pureed to about the consistency of baby food.

TO ROLL OUT, FILL, AND BAKE THE PIE: Remove the dough from refrigerator and roll it into a 12-inch circle. Place it in a 9½-inch pie plate, lightly pressing the dough into the dish and trimming the excess. Fold the overhanging dough under and lightly press the tines of a fork around the edge of the piecrust or use your thumb and knuckles to make a pattern.

Pour the filling into the crust and bake for 15 minutes, then reduce the temperature to 350°F and bake for an additional 45 minutes, or until a thin-bladed knife inserted into the center of the pie comes out clean. If the crust starts to brown too quickly, cover the crust with a strip of aluminum foil.

Remove the pie from the oven, place on a wire rack, and let cool completely, about 2 hours.

WHILE THE PIE IS COOLING, MAKE THE RED CURRY CREAM: By hand or using a stand mixer, whip the cream with the sugar until soft peaks form, about 3 minutes. Gently fold in the red curry paste, taking care not to deflate the whipped cream.

TO MAKE THE CANDIED THAI BASIL: Use a brush to wet both sides of each basil leaf with egg white. Sprinkle with sugar to cover each leaf evenly. As each leaf is coated, set it on a wire rack to dry for at least 2 hours or overnight.

TO SERVE: Slice the pie and serve with dollops of red curry cream and candied Thai basil.

ลูกแพร์เชื่อมชาเย็น

THAI TEA–POACHED PEARS

LOOK PEAR CHUAM CHAYEN

MAKES 6

Elegant pears take on the dark, smoky flavors and rich red color of Thai tea in this new fall classic, complemented by bittersweet chocolate, fragrant jasmine, and toasted coconut. It's not overly sweet, but earthy, and complex, and gets even better served on top of nutty, chewy sticky rice. Use a melon baller to core the pears while keeping their stems intact—this gives the pear a flatter base while poaching and makes for a more elegant presentation.

1 cup Thai tea powder

¾ cup sugar (more or less, to taste)

6 large Bosc pears, peeled and cored

Bittersweet Chocolate Ganache (recipe follows)

Toasted shredded unsweetened coconut (optional)

Bring 6 to 8 cups water to a boil in saucepan. Once boiling, stir in the Thai tea powder (or use an infuser) and sugar and immediately turn off the heat. Let the tea steep for 5 to 10 minutes.

Stand the peeled, cored pears in another tall pot and gently strain the steeped tea over the pears to cover. Cover the pot and turn the heat to medium. Poach the pears for 30 to 45 minutes, depending on size. The tea will turn the pears a deep, mahogany red.

When done, gently remove the pears from the poaching liquid and let cool.

Place the poached pears on serving plates and drizzle generously with Bittersweet Chocolate Ganache and sprinkle with coconut.

BITTERSWEET CHOCOLATE GANACHE

MAKES 3 CUPS

12 ounces bittersweet chocolate, roughly chopped; or 2 cups bittersweet chocolate chips

1 (13.5-ounce) can coconut milk

1 teaspoon jasmine extract

In a microwavable bowl, melt the chocolate and about one quarter of the coconut milk in a microwave oven for 2 to 3 minutes. Gently stir with a wooden spoon or spatula until well mixed.

Add the remaining coconut milk and the jasmine extract and stir until the ganache turns shiny.

เครื่องปรุง
CONDIMENTS

THE FOUR CLASSIC THAI CONDIMENTS

This ubiquitous quartet of condiments represents the four essential flavors that all Thai cuisine aspires to balance: sweet (*nam tan*—white or light brown sugar), salty (*nam pla*—fish sauce with garlic and lime), spicy (*prik pan*—ground red Thai chiles), and sour (*prik nam som*—Thai chiles in vinegar). Found across Thailand, these four seasonings are served exclusively alongside noodle dishes, with or without soup.

พริกน้ำส้ม

THAI CHILES IN VINEGAR
PRIK NAM SOM

MAKES ABOUT 1 CUP

1 cup distilled white vinegar

1 fresh red or green long Thai chile, sliced ¼-inch thick

To give the Thai long chiles a quick pickle, mix the two ingredients about 30 minutes before serving.

อาจาด

CUCUMBER RELISH

AJARD

MAKES ABOUT 3 CUPS

I have a vivid memory of my grandma criticizing a limp *ajard* we got from the market, explaining that the flavors of sour and sweet should dance with the crunchy cucumber. Always listen to Grandma Prapit!

As a refreshing side dish, this relish pairs especially well with Deep-Fried Thai Pork Tartines (page 126), Sweet Corn Fritters (page 189), or Pork Satay (page 24).

1 cup sugar

1 cup distilled white vinegar

1 cup sliced English cucumber (quartered and sliced thinly on the diagonal; about ½ cucumber)

¼ cup thinly sliced shallot

1 fresh long green or red Thai chile, thinly sliced on the diagonal

½ carrot, cut in half lengthwise and thinly sliced on the diagonal (optional)

In a medium saucepan, combine the sugar and vinegar. Place over medium heat, bring to a simmer, and stir continuously until the sugar is dissolved. Remove from the heat and set aside to cool.

In a medium bowl, toss together the cucumber, shallot, chile, and carrot, if using. Pour the vinegar mixture over the cucumber mixture and toss to coat evenly.

NOTE: I prefer using English or hothouse cucumbers because they're crunchier and less watery, so you don't have to remove the seeds.

น้ำปลาพริก

FISH SAUCE WITH CHILES

NAM PLA PRIK

MAKES ¼ CUP

This sauce elevates almost any good Thai dish to an excellent one, especially if you like your food a little spicy. I put it on top of rice and noodle dishes. The spiciness of the chiles satisfies the Thai in me. It's a quick and simple way to add a fresh punch of flavor.

¼ cup fish sauce

1 tablespoon thinly sliced fresh red Thai chile (⅛-inch rounds)

1 clove garlic, thinly sliced (optional)

Lime wedge

In a small bowl, combine the fish sauce, chile slices, and garlic, if using. Squeeze the lime wedge over the mixture and add the wedge to the sauce.

ข้าวคั่ว

TOASTED RICE POWDER

KHAO KHUA

MAKES ABOUT 1 CUP

This is a simple seasoning that adds an earthy, aromatic flavor to many northern Thai dishes and gives silky body to dipping sauces. Be certain to grind the rice finely to avoid a gritty texture.

½ cup uncooked sticky rice

¼ cup uncooked jasmine rice

1 (3-inch) piece galangal, sliced into thin coins

4 to 5 kaffir lime leaves

2 tablespoons chopped lemongrass

Toast all the ingredients a dry wok or skillet over low heat, gently stirring often until lightly colored and fragrant, about 8 minutes.

Remove from the heat to a plate and let cool. In a stone mortar, use the pestle to grind the ingredients to a fine powder (alternatively, grind the ingredients in a spice grinder). The powder will keep in an airtight container for up to 2 weeks.

ซอสหมัก

NGAM'S HOUSE MARINADE

SAUCE MAK

MAKES ABOUT 2 CUPS

This versatile marinade both tenderizes and flavors meat and can be used for chicken, pork, beef, or seafood. It will become your go-to recipe for summer grilling—trust me!

¼ cup mixed cilantro roots, cleaned, and cilantro stems and leaves

1 cup peeled garlic cloves

2 teaspoons whole white peppercorns

1 cup fish sauce

½ cup shaved palm sugar

1 cup oyster sauce

5 stalks lemongrass

2 tablespoons ground turmeric

1 teaspoon salt

Combine all the ingredients in a blender and blend until well combined.

น้ำพริกแกงแดง

RED CURRY PASTE

NAM PRIK GAENG DAENG

MAKES ABOUT ½ CUP

There are many varieties of red curry in Thai cuisine—*kang dang*, *kang ped*, *panang*, and more. This is a standard red curry adaptable to all the recipes in this book. There's nothing as satisfying as making your own curry paste. The hard part used to be getting the right ingredients, but these days they're easier to find than ever, especially online. Kaffir lime peel is actually more authentic, if also much harder to find, than the leaves, but both add the right flavor.

5 dried red long Thai chiles

2 teaspoons coriander seeds

2 teaspoons cumin seeds

1 teaspoon whole white peppercorns

1 (1-inch) piece galangal, thinly sliced

2 stalks lemongrass (bottom 2 to 3 inches), bruised and thinly sliced

5 kaffir lime leaves; or the whole peel of 1 kaffir lime

3 cilantro roots, cleaned

8 cloves garlic, coarsely chopped (about ¼ cup)

3 small shallots, coarsely chopped (about ¼ cup)

Place the dried chiles in a bowl and add warm water to cover. Leave to soften for about 15 minutes. Wearing kitchen gloves (do not use bare hands when working with chiles), remove the chiles from the water and squeeze out excess water. Set the rehydrated chiles aside—they give the curry its distinctive red color.

Toast the coriander seeds, cumin seeds, and white peppercorns in a small skillet over very low heat until fragrant, 1 to 2 minutes. Grind using a stone mortar and pestle. (Alternatively, use a spice grinder and stir the spices into the paste after it's been ground.)

Add the rehydrated chiles and pound into a rough paste, 2 to 3 minutes. Add the galangal, lemongrass, kaffir lime leaves or peel, cilantro roots, garlic, and shallots and continue pounding into a smooth paste, about 20 more minutes.

NOTE: In the absence of a stone mortar and pestle, you can make this curry paste in a blender, adding up to ½ cup coconut milk to help break down the fibrous ingredients.

น้ำพริกแกงเขียวหวาน

GREEN CURRY PASTE

NAM PRIK GAENG KHIAW WAN

MAKES ABOUT 1 CUP

Gang kiaw wan breaks down into three words: *gang*, "curry"; *kiaw*, "green"; and *wan*, "sweet." When I'm eating green curry, I always look for that beautiful army green hue from the crushed Thai herbs and a sweet, creamy flavor from good-quality coconut milk and a touch a palm sugar. Heat is not the main attraction—it plays a supporting role in this fragrant curry.

It's important to use a mortar and pestle here instead of chopping because when working with herbs that contain aromatic oils, bruising (which is what the mortar and pestle do) releases more of the oils than chopping. Plus, it's therapeutic to pound them! If you don't have a stone mortar, you can blend everything in a blender; just add about ½ cup coconut milk to help cut up the fibrous ingredients.

1 teaspoon coriander seeds

1 teaspoon cumin seeds

1 teaspoon whole white peppercorns

3 to 4 green bird's eye chiles, chopped

2 long green Thai chiles, chopped

1 (1-inch) piece galangal, thinly sliced

2 stalks lemongrass (bottom 2 to 3 inches), bruised and thinly sliced

5 kaffir lime leaves or 1 piece kaffir lime peel

3 cilantro roots, cleaned

8 cloves garlic, coarsely chopped (about ¼ cup)

2 to 3 small shallots, coarsely chopped (about ¼ cup)

Toast the coriander seeds, cumin seeds, and white peppercorns in a small skillet over very low heat until fragrant, 1 to 2 minutes. Grind using a stone mortar and pestle, or spice grinder.

In the same mortar, add the two types of chiles and pound with the spices until they break apart. Add the galangal, lemongrass, kaffir lime leaves, cilantro roots, garlic, and shallots and continue pounding into a smooth paste, about 20 minutes.

NOTE: Many traditional Thai curries also include shrimp paste, to add further sweet and savory depth of flavor. I prefer to omit it, but if you want to add shrimp paste to yours, simply stir 2 teaspoons into the finished green curry paste after pounding in the mortar and pestle.

น้ำพริกผัดพริกขิง

PRIK KHING CURRY PASTE

NAM PRIK PAD PRIK KHING

MAKES ABOUT 1 CUP

This is another version of red curry that I love. Less creamy, as recipes calling for this particular curry paste don't usually contain coconut milk, it has a brighter citrus fragrance perfect for light dishes, especially seafood. To maximize its fresh flavors and bright color, *Prik Khing* Curry Paste should be used right away.

5 dried red long Thai chiles, or to taste

1 (1-inch) piece galangal, sliced into coins

2 stalks lemongrass (bottom 2 to 3 inches), bruised and roughly chopped

3 whole kaffir lime leaves; or 1 kaffir lime peel

2 cilantro roots, cleaned

10 cloves garlic, coarsely chopped

2 to 3 small shallots, coarsely chopped (about ¼ cup)

2 tablespoons dried shrimp

1 teaspoon shrimp paste

Place the dried chiles in a bowl and add warm water to cover. Leave to soften for about 15 minutes. Wearing kitchen gloves (do not use bare hands when working with chiles), remove the chiles from the water and squeeze out excess water.

Using a stone mortar and pestle, pound the chiles, galangal, lemongrass, kaffir lime leaves or peel, cilantro roots, garlic, and shallots for 20 to 25 minutes to form a smooth paste. Add the dried shrimp and shrimp paste and stir to combine. Or combine the paste ingredients in a blender with up to ½ cup vegetable oil and process until smooth.

น้ำพริกอ่อง

NORTHERN-STYLE PORK AND CHERRY TOMATO RELISH

NAM PRIK ONG

SERVES 4 TO 6

This relish—ground pork mixed with chile paste and tomatoes and seasoned with Thai miso—is a famous dish from northern Thailand. It's typically served as a dip with fresh vegetables such as cucumbers, carrots, wing beans, and/or cabbage. Steamed cabbage, cauliflower, and long green beans also work well, as do crispy pork rinds.

5 dried long red Thai chiles

1 shallot, thinly sliced (about ¼ cup)

¼ cup chopped garlic

2 stalks lemongrass, sliced

1 tablespoon chopped galangal

¼ cup Thai miso

2 tablespoons vegetable oil

1 pound ground pork

1 cup halved cherry tomatoes

1 cup Thai Chicken Stock (page 236) or water

1 teaspoon salt

1 tablespoon fish sauce

1 tablespoon palm sugar

1 to 2 sprigs cilantro, coarsely chopped

1 scallion, thinly sliced

Place the dried chiles in a bowl and add warm water to cover. Leave to soften for about 15 minutes. Wearing kitchen gloves (do not use bare hands when working with chiles), remove the chiles from the water and squeeze out excess water.

In a stone mortar, combine the hydrated chiles, the shallot, garlic, lemongrass, galangal, and Thai miso and pound with a pestle into a smooth paste, 15 to 20 minutes. Set aside.

Heat the oil in a large sauté pan over medium heat. Add the paste and sauté, stirring, until fragrant, about 3 minutes. Add the ground pork and cook, stirring, for 5 minutes, or until the pork is mostly cooked through. Stir in the tomatoes, then add the stock and bring to a boil. Add the salt, fish sauce, and sugar, lower the heat to maintain a simmer, and simmer for 10 minutes, until just slightly reduced and the flavors blend. Transfer to a bowl and garnish with the cilantro and scallion.

กระเทียมเจียว

FRIED GARLIC

GRATIAM JIAW

MAKES ABOUT ½ CUP

This crispy garlic is quite popular in many Thai dishes, especially noodle dishes such as Boat Noodles (page 143), Rice Noodles with Cherry Tomatoes and Pork (page 49), and Pork *Laab* (page 82).

1 cup vegetable oil

1 whole head garlic, peeled, cloves finely chopped

Combine the oil and garlic in a small saucepan over low heat. Stir constantly with a wooden spoon for about 3 minutes, just until the garlic turns a light golden brown. Your nose will also tell you when it's ready—your kitchen will fill with the rich aroma of toasted garlic. Watch—and sniff—closely, as the garlic can go from perfect to burned heartbreakingly fast if you turn your back. Once it turns golden and smells right, remove from the heat immediately and let the hot oil finish the job.

NAM JIM TALAY

NAM JIM TAO JIAW

NAM JIM GAI

NAM JIM JIAW

NAM PLA PRIK

NAM JIM BAW BIA

น้ำจิ้มปอเปี๊ยะ

ORANGE-GINGER DIPPING SAUCE

NAM JIM BAW BIA

MAKES ABOUT 1 CUP

This may not be a traditional Thai sauce, but ginger and orange are a classic combination I build on to create a bright dipping sauce. We serve this daily at Ngam with *baw bia* (page 186). The tangy ginger complements the earthy mushrooms and vermicelli noodles and the acid in the orange juice and vinegar are perfect with anything crispy.

Grated zest and juice of 2 large oranges (about 1 cup)

2 tablespoons finely chopped ginger

2 tablespoons distilled white vinegar

2 tablespoons granulated sugar

1 tablespoon palm sugar

Pinch of salt

Combine all the ingredients in a small saucepan, place over medium heat, and bring to a simmer. Simmer, stirring, just until the sugar is dissolved and the flavors meld, about 5 minutes (boiling will turn the citrus juice bitter, so don't turn your back for long). Remove from the heat and let cool before serving.

น้ำจิ้มแจ่ว

ISSAN-STYLE DIPPING SAUCE

NAM JIM JIAW

MAKES ABOUT 1 CUP

Zab is a Thai word often used to describe the cuisine of northern Thailand, for which there isn't quite an exact English translation—it suggests a flavor that's equally spicy, sour, and savory, and it definitely applies to this simple fresh dipping sauce. Just combine the ingredients and you're ready, no cooking required! Serve this with the Issan-style *shabu shabu* (page 160), the Happy Tiger (page 208), or any recipe you want to enhance with a delicious tangy sauce.

½ cup fish sauce

¼ cup lime juice

1 tablespoon Toasted Rice Powder (page 227)

1 tablespoon *Laab* Chile (page 83), or to taste (see Note)

1 shallot, thinly sliced (about 2 tablespoons)

1 tablespoon finely chopped cilantro

Combine all the ingredients in a bowl and stir until well mixed.

NOTE: You can substitute plain red Thai chile powder for the *Laab* Chile.

น้ำจิ้มไก่

SPICY TAMARIND DIPPING SAUCE

NAM JIM GAI

MAKES ABOUT 2 CUPS

½ cup vegetable oil

10 cloves garlic, coarsely chopped

5 dried red Thai chiles, roughly crushed
   into large pieces

⅔ cup tamarind concentrate

1 cup palm sugar

½ cup fish sauce

Heat the oil in a medium saucepan over medium-high heat. Add the garlic and chiles and cook, stirring gently, until fragrant, about 2 minutes. Add the tamarind concentrate, sugar, and fish sauce and cook, stirring, until the sugar is dissolved. Bring to a boil, then lower the heat to low and cook until it reaches the consistency of a thick glaze, about 15 minutes. Remove from the heat and let cool to room temperature. Transfer to a blender and blend until smooth.

น้ำจิ้มเต้าเจี้ยว

THAI MISO DIPPING SAUCE

NAM JIM TAO JIAW

MAKES ABOUT 2 CUPS

Full of the salty, sweet flavors of Thai miso, sugar, and ginger, this thick, dark, no-cook sauce elevates the simple poached chicken and aromatic rice in Chicken and Rice (page 67) or any light-flavored dish.

¾ cup Thai miso

½ cup sugar

¾ cup lime juice

¼ cup black sweet soy sauce

¼ cup chopped ginger

3 to 4 cloves garlic, chopped

5 to 6 fresh red Thai chiles, chopped

In a blender, combine all the ingredients and blend until well combined.

น้ำจิ้มทะเล

SPICY LIME AND CHILE SAUCE

NAM JIM TALAY

MAKES ABOUT 2 CUPS

There's nothing better than perfectly fresh seafood, but I admit I love it most when paired with this spicy, tangy dipping sauce. Without question, this is my go-to sauce when it comes to anything seafood, so try it with any favorite dish of yours. Somehow it makes every bite better than the last.

2 tablespoons chopped fresh red Thai chiles

5 cloves garlic, roughly chopped

1 cup palm sugar

1 cup fish sauce

1 cup lime juice

In a stone mortar, use a pestle to crush the chiles and garlic until they form a fine (and very aromatic!) paste. Add the sugar, fish sauce, and lime juice and use the pestle to mix everything until well combined.

NOTE: Blend the ingredients in a blender if you don't have a stone mortar and pestle; just be sure the sugar is shaved finely to avoid damaging the mechanism.

น้ำต้มกระดูกไก่

THAI CHICKEN STOCK

NAM TOM KRADOOK GAI

MAKES ABOUT 6 QUARTS

Good stock makes good soup. This simple chicken stock balances the spicy aromas of cilantro roots and black pepper with sweetness from a generous amount of daikon.

1 whole farm-raised chicken (3 to 4½ pounds)

1 pound daikon (about 2 medium roots), peeled and cut into 2-inch slices

10 cilantro roots, cleaned

1 whole head garlic, cut in half

1 teaspoon whole black peppercorns

Combine all the ingredients in a large stockpot. Add cold water to cover, about 8 quarts, and bring to a boil. Reduce the heat to low to maintain a low simmer and simmer, uncovered, for about 3 hours, skimming any foam that rises to the top as needed.

Remove from the heat and let cool, then strain through a colander lined with cheesecloth. Discard the solids or use the boiled chicken in another recipe, such as Chicken and Rice (page 67). Store the stock in a covered container in the refrigerator for up to 3 days or freeze up to 3 months.

น้ำต้มกระดูกหมู

PORK STOCK

NAM TOM KRADOOK MOO

MAKE ABOUT 2 QUARTS

For me the quality of a pork stock is determined by its depth of flavor, which is why I use ribs here—the bones contribute both flavor and collagen to help thicken the stock. This is especially important when you are using your stock as a base for noodle dishes—it's key to getting that true Thai flavor.

2 pounds baby back pork ribs

8 ounces daikon (about 1 medium root), peeled and cut into 2-inch slices

10 cilantro roots, cleaned

1 whole head garlic, cut in half

1 tablespoon whole black peppercorns

1 tablespoon salt

3 tablespoons mushroom sauce

⅓ cup brown sugar

In a stockpot, combine 3 quarts water, the ribs, daikon, cilantro roots, garlic, and peppercorns. Place over high heat and bring to a boil. Lower the heat to low to maintain a low simmer, skimming any foam that rises to the top as needed. Add the salt, mushroom sauce, and brown sugar and simmer, uncovered, for about 3 hours. At this point, the broth will have a rich bone marrow flavor. Remove from the heat and let cool, then strain through a colander lined with cheesecloth. Discard the solids and store the stock in a covered container in the refrigerator for up to 3 days or freeze for up to 3 months.

น้ำซุปทะเล

THAI SEAFOOD STOCK

NAM SOUP TALAY

MAKES ABOUT 2½ QUARTS

When it comes to seafood, I like adding lots of herbs—kaffir lime leaves, galangal, and lemongrass, plus the classic garlic, cilantro roots, and peppercorns. The broth is rich and fragrant and will give any seafood dish unbeatable depth of flavor.

Heads, shells, and tails from about 2 pounds lobster or shrimp

16 whole kaffir lime leaves

1 (4-inch) piece galangal, cut into thick coins

4 stalks lemongrass, cut into 4-inch lengths, bruised

5 cilantro roots, cleaned

1 whole head garlic, cut in half lengthwise

1 tablespoon whole black peppercorns

Combine all the ingredients in a stockpot. Add cold water to cover, about 3 quarts, and bring to a boil. Reduce the heat to low to maintain a low simmer and simmer, uncovered, for about 1 hour, skimming any foam that rises to the top as needed. Remove from the heat and let cool, then strain through a colander lined with cheesecloth. Discard the solids and store the stock in a covered container in the refrigerator for up to 3 days for freeze for up to 3 months.

น้ำยำ

SIMPLE THAI SALAD DRESSING

NAM YUM

MAKES ABOUT 1½ CUPS

I prefer the taste of honey in my dressing, but if you choose to use sugar, make a simple syrup by mixing the sugar with hot water until dissolved and cool the syrup before adding the rest of the ingredients. If you're using palm sugar, pound the chiles and sugar together in the mortar. I use this, with a little added garlic, on Grandma's Sunny-Side-Up Eggs (page 26), and with a little extra heat for my Spicy Kale and Mushroom Salad (page 196). Once you find the balance of salty, sweet, sour, and spicy you prefer, you'll have made this recipe your own.

2 chopped fresh red Thai chiles, or to taste

½ cup fish sauce

½ cup lime juice

¼ cup honey or simple syrup (see Note)

In a stone mortar, pound the chiles with a pestle to bruise them. In a small bowl, whisk together the fish sauce, lime juice, honey, and bruised chiles until the honey is dissolved.

The dressing is best fresh, but it keeps in a covered container in the refrigerator for up to a week.

NOTE: Simple syrup is as easy to make as it sounds. Simply combine 1 part granulated sugar and 1 part water in a saucepan over medium heat and stir until the sugar dissolves, about 5 minutes. Cool and store in the refrigerator to stir into drinks or recipes. See page 175 for other flavored variations on simple syrup.

INGREDIENTS GLOSSARY

Banana blossoms

Betel leaves

Chile jam

As the popularity of Thai cuisine grows, it's easier than ever to find most of these ingredients outside of Thailand. Seek out a trustworthy Asian grocery in your city's Chinatown and it will likely have a wide selection. If you live in a warmer region, try your local farmers' market, as more and more Asian fruits, greens, and vegetables are grown stateside. Many sauces, spices, and other pantry items can be found online—try importfood.com or templeofthai.com for a range of authentic Thai groceries, and kalustyans.com has a wide variety of curry powders, peppercorns, and other spices.

ASIAN MEATBALLS / *luk chin*

Savory Asian-style meatballs are made from a variety of minced protein, including beef, chicken, fish, pork, and squid, mixed with seasonings and rice flour into a paste, then rolled into small, dense meatballs. Most can be easily found fully cooked and frozen in Asian groceries or markets, ready to be blanched and added to hot soups or noodle dishes.

BANANA BLOSSOMS / *hua plee*

Also called banana hearts, the edible flower of the banana tree is a popular vegetable in Thai cuisine. They're big for flowers, almost the size and shape of a small football, and a deep purple color. Often compared to artichokes, another flower in the vegetable family, banana blossoms must be peeled and cored similarly, and, like artichoke hearts, discolor quickly once exposed to air unless used right away or treated with lemon or lime juice. Their subtle, slightly bitter flavor mellows and sweetens with cooking.

BETEL LEAVES / *bai chaploo*

Dark, glossy green heart-shaped betel leaves come from the evergreen betel vine. They're traditionally used to wrap small bites such as *miang kam* (page 23) or food for the grill. Betel leaves are fresh, herbaceous additions to simple salads, and I like to stir them into curries, where they add peppery, savory flavor—try them in the Southern-Style Mussel Curry (page 108). My dad always says to eat Green Papaya Salad (page 139) or anything spicy or sour with betel leaves, as they can help settle your stomach and freshen your breath.

CHILE JAM / *nam prik pao*

This is a sweet and spicy condiment made from dried shrimp, garlic, shallots, and chiles and seasoned with fish sauce, palm sugar, and tamarind. Often stirred into curry dishes such as Sautéed Crab with Egg and Curry Sauce (page 115), it's also a popular seasoning on its own—try it over rice or on a piece of toast.

Cilantro

Culantro

Eggplants

CHINESE CELERY / *keun chai*

Prized more for the clean, refreshing flavor of its thin stems and leaves than its crunch, Chinese celery is a popular addition to Thai soups and salads. If difficult to find in Asian groceries, the tender, inner stalks and leaves of regular celery hearts are an easy substitute.

CILANTRO ROOT / *raag pak chee*

While cilantro is well known, the roots of the cilantro plant are also popular in Thai dishes for their punch of fresh, clean, herby flavor. When paired with garlic and pepper, they make a great marinade and stock base and are a vital ingredient in curry pastes. The flavor of the root is more concentrated, so to use the aboveground stems and leaves in its place, you will need the whole bunch—finely chop all stems and leaves and proceed with the recipe.

CULANTRO / *bai pak chee farang*

Found in both traditional Caribbean and Southeast Asian cuisine, culantro is a bright green leafy herb often referred to as sawtooth mint or long coriander, with a bright, herbal flavor similar to cilantro and mint, but more intense. Its long leaves have distinctive zigzag edges and retain their crunchy texture during both cooking and drying, making culantro good for both long-simmering dishes such as Pork *Laab* (page 82) and used fresh as an assertive garnish or addition to dipping sauces or salads such as Chiang Mai Raw Beef Salad (page 35).

EGGPLANT / *makrua*

Eggplant appears in many Thai recipes, from salads and *som tum* to curries and stir-fries. Long eggplant (*makrua yao*) are very similar to Italian or slender Japanese eggplant and come in both green and bright purple. Smaller, with a crunchier bite and slightly bitter flavor that many Thais enjoy fresh or added to quick curries, is the apple eggplant (*makrua praw*), about the size of a Ping-Pong ball. These oxidize quickly once cut, so keep them in lime or lemon water until ready to use. The smallest of all, almost the size of chickpeas, are Thai pea eggplants (*makrua poorng*), which can be hard to find in the United States outside of Asian markets. Their juicy, almost-sour flavor perks up northern-style braises and curries, such as Stir-Fried Wild Boar with Red Curry (page 58), but either apple eggplant or even Japanese eggplant can work in a pinch.

Galangal

Green papaya

Krachai

FISH SAUCE / *nam pla*

Another of the cornerstones of Thai cooking, fish sauce is made from drying and fermenting small fish, such as anchovies, to make a pungent salty, savory sauce that's added to almost everything, from salads and noodle dishes to curries and even dipping sauces. Good-quality fish sauce should have a clear, amber color and a fresh, briny-sweet aroma. *Pla la* sauce from northeastern Thailand (see Green Papaya Salad on page 139) and Boodoo dressing (see Grandma's Rice Bowl on page 120) are both popular salty condiments made with fermented fish.

GALANGAL / *kha*

Galangal looks very similar to ginger—it's from the same family and is often called blue ginger, though its aroma and flavor are not alike, galangal having a peppery, mustardy flavor compared to sweet, spicy ginger, and the two are not used interchangeably. Galangal is also tougher and woodier than ginger and does not soften as much during cooking, so it is usually julienned, minced, or pounded into a curry paste. Fresh galangal is relatively easy to find, especially in Asian markets, but frozen is recommended over dried.

GREEN PAPAYA / *malako*

You can find unripe (green) papaya year round in Asian and specialty supermarkets. Once peeled, the fruit is easy to slice or shred. Its crunchy texture and fresh, neutral flavor make a perfect base for many pungent, spicy salads and slaws, such as Green Papaya Salad (page 139) and air-dried as a raw stand-in for rice noodles in *pad thai* (page 201).

KRACHAI

This relative of ginger is also called "finger roots," as it often resembles a long-fingered hand. Peeled and diced or grated like ginger, it has a similar sharp, sweet flavor and is often used to balance out the strong, gamey flavors of boar or lamb, as in Stir-Fried Wild Boar with Red Curry (page 58), and pairs well with seafood, as in Dancing Calamari (page 111). If you can't find it fresh, a frozen version is good but must be drained of excess water after thawing or your dish will be diluted.

LEMONGRASS / *takrai*

As the name suggests, lemongrass is a stalk of long grass with a floral, citrus flavor, used dried, powdered, and fresh in many dishes. The yellow-green outside is firm and woody, but the bright white middle and purple innermost layers remain tender and are the most fragrant. Similar to green onions, typically only the tender, light-colored 2 or 3 inches of the

Long beans

Mint

Pickled mustard

inner stalk closest to the root are chopped and added to curry pastes or stir-fry dishes, but the rest can be used in tea, to flavor soups or stocks, or bruised and used as an aromatic basting brush for grilled dishes.

LONG BEANS OR YARD-LONG BEANS / *toor fak yao*

Delicious either fresh or cooked—long beans are steamed and used as a side with *nam prik* dipping sauce, stir-fried with *prik khing* and crispy pork belly or calamari, or chopped and added raw to *som tum*. You can find long beans in most Asian grocery stores, as it's a common ingredient in Chinese, Malaysian, and Indonesian cuisines. Fresh local green or wax beans or even haricots verts have a similar clean, vegetal flavor if not the same firm bite.

MINT / *bai saranae*

Like basil, cilantro, and lemongrass, mint is a staple herb in Thai cooking, its fresh sweetness brightening spicy dishes, rich soups, and salads. Bamboo or Vietnamese mint (*bai pak pai*) has spicier herbal notes that I like in stronger flavored dishes, such as Pork *Laab* (page 82) and my Rustic Chicken Soup (page 193).

PALM SUGAR / *nam tan peep*

Made from the sap of the palm tree, palm sugar is the most common traditional sweetener in Thai cooking and has a round, deep flavor with some molasses notes. Because of the heat in Thailand, palm sugar tends to be softer in texture, sometimes almost like a caramel. In the United States, palm sugar is usually found in dense, solid cubes that should be finely shaved or chopped before using.

PICKLED MUSTARD / *pak gard dong*

Not the prepared, bright yellow sauce we're accustomed to, *pak gard dong* refers to jarred mustard greens that have been pickled with salt and sugar. The heart of the greens usually retains its bright yellow-green color, while the outer leaves turn a darker brown. Acidic and salty, pickled mustard is popular as a condiment to curries and noodle dishes, such as *Khao Soy* (page 41), or can be made into a bracing salad to accompany Late-Night Rice Porridge (page 129).

SHRIMP PASTE / *kapi*

Like fish sauce or even miso, shrimp paste is a common ingredient in Thai cuisine that adds *umami*, a deep, savory flavor note, here both salty and a little sweet from the shrimp. It's a key ingredient in curry pastes and is used often in dipping sauces.

Tamarind

Thai basil

Thai chiles

TAMARIND / *nam ma kam piak*

The sweet and tangy flavor of tamarind features in many traditional Thai dishes, from sweets to dipping sauces to *pad thai* (page 201). Jarred juice or pulp can be easily found in Asian markets but is often too weak and watery. Solid, seedless tamarind pulp is also sold in blocks from which you can make your own concentrate: Simply dissolve a solid 14-ounce block in about 8 cups warm water, squeezing the mixture with your hands to separate the stringy veins and seed-covering membranes from the smooth, sweet pulp (discard solids). Homemade tamarind concentrate will keep for up to one week in the refrigerator or indefinitely in the freezer.

THAI BASIL / *bai horapa*

Thai basil has such a sweet aromatic scent that it's sometimes simply called "sweet basil." One of the main ingredients of Thai cuisine, basil goes into curries both red and green, drunken noodles, and stir-fries. Holy basil (*bai krapow*) has a more fiery character, all the better for spicy dishes like Crispy Catfish with *Prik Khing* Sauce (page 154). The elegant, undeniably citrusy aroma of lemon basil (*bai mangluck*) elevates the flavors in stir-fries like Banana Blossom and Shrimp Curry (page 51).

THAI CHILES / *prik kee noo*

When recipes call simply for "Thai chiles," they mean *prik kee noo*, the basic small red or green chile peppers added to many traditional dishes. Their flavor is more piquant than hot—sharp, peppery, and aromatic. *Prik chee fah*, or Thai long chiles, are just that—longer and not usually quite as hot; these are often used for marinating in vinegar as a popular garnish. They come in a variety of colors, from green to red and light orange. *Prik kee noo* and *prik chee fah* are used both fresh and dried. Dried red Thai chiles are one of the four classic Thai condiments (page 225) and are a key ingredient in Red Curry Paste (page 229). Sometimes called Indian long pepper or Indonesian long pepper, both fresh and dried *dee plee* peppers add rich flavor and heat to traditional dishes such as *laab* (page 82). They grow about an inch long on a flowering vine, and, like raspberries or strawberries, have their seeds on the outside.

THAI MISO / *tao jiaw*

Soybeans fermented with flour, salt, and water, miso is a traditional Asian ingredient and popular source of the savory, satisfying flavor umami. Its salty-sweet flavor makes a great dipping sauce for Chicken and Rice (see page 67) and adds depth to stir fries and noodle dishes, such as My Favorite Noodle Dish in the Whole World (page 49). Thai miso can be found as a paste or dried, in discs 3 to 4 inches across called *toor nao*, used commonly in northern Thai dishes.

Thai miso

Turmeric

Young peppercorns

THAI TEA POWDER / *phong cha yen*

Thai iced tea is a refreshing, world-famous beverage that gets its distinctive sweet, aromatic flavors from a blend of black Ceylon tea leaves, vanilla, cinnamon, and star anise, as well as other spices, in various combinations. Besides offering the drink to my guests at Ngam, I like using the earthy, smoky-sweet tea in cocktails, such as my Iced Tea-Tini (page 180) and as a spicy poaching liquid for Thai Tea–Poached Pears (page 222). Thai iced tea mixes and powdered blends are easy to find in Asian markets and online; traditionally the characteristic bright orange color of Thai iced tea comes from food coloring, but all-natural versions include no dyes or chemicals.

TURMERIC / *kamin*

This beautiful bright orange root has a long history in Thai culture and figures in many traditional recipes, medicinal home remedies, and even cosmetics. It's an essential ingredient in most southern Thai curry pastes and powders and lends its distinctive yellow-orange color to many dishes. The roots are small, about the size of a pinky finger. Just like ginger, the peel is brown and very fragile and must be removed before grating, dicing, or pounding into a paste. Fresh turmeric is easy to find, but good-quality dried ground turmeric can be a fine substitute. Note that dried turmeric is typically stronger than fresh.

YOUNG PEPPERCORNS / *prik Thai*

Native to Thailand and Southeast Asia, pepper was the primary source of spice in Thai cuisine prior to the introduction of chile peppers by Europeans—hence its name, *prik thai* ("Thai pepper"). Fresh peppercorns look like tight sprigs of bright green berries, which eventually ripen and turn red. Varieties such as Tellicherry are dried in the sun to make black peppercorns; others, such as Muntok or Sarawak, are then washed in a solution that removes the darkened and dried outer layers of the berry, leaving smooth white peppercorns. Young, fresh peppercorns, which haven't been allowed to ripen on the vine, remain a popular addition to many traditional dishes, where their subtler, more fragrant, less intense heat is preferred over that of *prik kee noo* or *prik chee fah*. Found fresh in warm climates or specialty markets, they're sometimes available frozen (freezing turns their color black) or jarred in brine (rinse before using).

INDEX

ACKNOWLEDGMENTS

This book is a true labor of love. Most importantly, thank you God for creating a world full of delicious flavors and for showing me what love is. Thank you, Rizzoli, for giving me this wonderful opportunity.

My wonderful team: Jono Jarrett, my editor, you are a dream to work with! Thank you for your patience and wisdom. To my talented team of photographers, Noah Fecks and Paul Wagtouicz, thanks for narrating my life through your lenses. Jenn Kim, my producer, thanks for taking care of all logistics and travel details. Rob Harmon, thanks for taking care of my face and hair, and for being a source of positive energy every day that we shot together in Thailand. Rebecca Sunde, thank you for assisting me throughout the journey. You are my angel! Alyssa and Paul Hoppe, thank you for your creative eyes. Tina Ujlaki, thank you for helping me with your wisdom. To everyone at Rizzoli and especially to Lynne Yeamans, thank you for your patience and skill in turning my dream into such a beautiful book.

Thank you also to my Ngam family—Sung Ko, Andy Pirgousis, and Sung Choi, and all of my kitchen staff, especially Chalermpan Insuwan, Aditya Kangutkar, and Supakorn Srijaroenporn, for testing recipes. And to Billy Mallas, my GM and the front of house team, thank you for taking care of Ngam while I was gone making this book. Without your support, this would have not happened.

Our incredible trip to Thailand to photograph the book could never have happened without the generosity of so many: In Chiang Mai, thank you to the entire village of Bann Nong Yang in Sansai Chiang Mai. We will be forever grateful for your hospitality. Thank you to Khun Surachai Leosawasthiphong for allowing us to use the unlimited resources at The Gallery, your beautiful restaurant. Thank you, Nong Ake, for assisting us with everything that we needed, and thank you to the Suvanish family of Manit Travel who took care of every domestic detail for us.

In Bangkok, thank you to Khun Vannee, Khun Apivat, and Geoffrey and Jarrod Sivayathorn of Sivatel Hotel for your hospitality and kindness. Karaoke with a view of downtown Bangkok is truly unforgettable. And to the whole Sivatel Hotel team. Ekarin Yusuksomboom, you are talented and we love you so much! Thank you for opening up your kitchen and taking us around town.

In southern Thailand, thank you to Khun Noppadol Prasertkul for hosting us at your beautiful villa, the Black Pearl (blackpearlphuket.com), with a special thank you to P Kiaw, the housekeeper, and Panda, the house dog. Nong Nid Waranid Meejinda, thank you so much to you and your team for assisting us.

To my friends and family in New York and across the globe—Dorothy & John McDermott, Rebecca Gibbons, Ruth Kwak, Pam Headen, Debbie Ecker, Tracy Marshall and Micheal Gutskowski, Patricia DeWit, Easton and Olga Rankine, Nic Evans and Brian Mahoney, and more—thank you for everything, from lending hands and phone calls to all kinds of support helping me get here. You all have helped me build my dream. I am forever grateful.

Last but not least, I want to thank my mom and dad for allowing me to pursue my dream. Chy, you are such a brother—thanks for believing in me. Kwan, thanks for assisting us on set at home. To you and the rest of my family—Aunt Aoy, Tuang, Aunt Tookta, Aunt Add, and, most importantly, my grandma, thank you for inspiring me to cook. Thank you for passing along the courage to believe anything is possible, especially in the kitchen.

First published in the United States of America in 2015
by Rizzoli International Publications, Inc.
300 Park Avenue South
New York, NY 10010
www.rizzoliusa.com

Photographs © Noah Fecks and Paul Wagtouicz

Design by Lynne Yeamans

2015 2016 2017 2018 / 10 9 8 7 6 5 4 3 2 1

Distributed in the U.S. trade by Random House, New York

Printed in China

ISBN-13: 978-0-8478-4623-8
Library of Congress Catalog Control Number: 2015935952